DUAL IMAGE
APPLIQUÉ

Dilys Fronks

American Quilter's Society
P. O. Box 3290 • Paducah, KY 42002-3290
www.AmericanQuilter.com

Located in Paducah, Kentucky, the American Quilter's Society (AQS) is dedicated to promoting the accomplishments of today's quilters. Through its publications and events, AQS strives to honor today's quiltmakers and their work and to inspire future creativity and innovation in quiltmaking.

Executive Book Editor: Andi Milam Reynolds
Senior Book Editor: Linda Baxter Lasco
Copy Editor: Chrystal Abhalter
Graphic Design: Julie Sartain
Cover Design: Michael Buckingham
Quilt Photography: Charles R. Lynch
How-to Photography: Roger Fronks

Additional copies of this book may be ordered from the American Quilter's Society, PO Box 3290, Paducah, KY 42002-3290, or online at www.AmericanQuilter.com.

Text © 2010, Author, Dilys Fronks
Artwork © 2010, American Quilter's Society

Library of Congress Cataloging-in-Publication Data

Fronks, Dilys A.
  Dual image appliqué / by Dilys Fronks.
     p. cm.
  ISBN 978-1-57432-673-4
  1. Quilting--Patterns. 2. Machine appliqué--Patterns.
3. Mirror images.
I. Title.
  TT835.F588 2010
  746.44'5--dc22
                                          2010037808

COVER: BOSTON FALL WALLHANGING, detail, made by the author. Full quilt on page 68.

DEDICATION

For my mother, Doris Osmotherley (née Owen) still sewing at 94 years. For my granddaughter Ella Rose Anderson—yet to sew at 1 year.

THANKS

To Roger, for his cheery and patient support, and excellent photography.

To May Reaney, for challenging my waste of fabric and kick-starting this book.

To my quilting chums and contributors: Dot Aellen, Judith Ayton, Helen Bailey, June Barker, Pauline Brown, Jennifer Ellis, Brenda Farnhill, Val Jones, Kath Lloyd, Eunice Lord, Jane Hadfield, Florine Schultz Johnson, Liz Pedley, May Reaney, Beth Stephenson, Iris Taylor, Celia McTeer, and Ruth Wallett.

To AQS: As an established author, I am delighted to team up with AQS for the first time. They have assisted me in my endeavor to present this teaching book in a clear, concise, and sympathetic way. I would specifically like to thank my own wonderful editorial team: Andi Reynolds and Linda Lasco.

TABLE OF CONTENTS

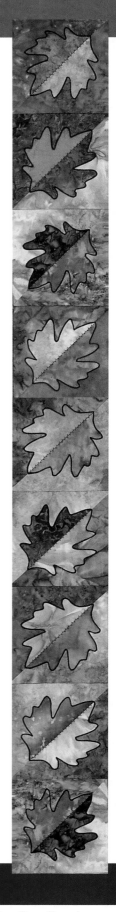

PREFACE ▶ Dual Image Appliqué Who's It For?

Dual Image Appliqué is for everyone!

My dual image appliqué technique is suitable for beginners who are just starting their journey into machine appliqué. The comprehensive section on machine stitching includes clear instructions on signing on and off, convex and concave curves, and inward and outward points. The heart Taster Block (page 17) is a manageable size for learning and practicing the machine sewing skills in a series of logical steps. From these simple beginnings, the appealing projects increase in degree of difficulty to take the reader on a journey through pattern, color, and proficiency.

The more experienced stitchers will find much to interest them in the way this novel method is used and developed, with its speedy application and glorious use of colors. The original projects are presented in an interesting and stimulating way to encourage readers to think beyond the normal way of doing their quilts.

Teachers are sure to find it an excellent resource book, with its structured, step-by-step layout, where illustrations and text show the way clearly through the method and projects. There are plenty of tips so no one gets lost along the way.

Whoever you are, this book is definitely for you!

INTRODUCTION ▶

BLUE HAWAII, 42" x 42"
a positive/negative appearance

The seeds of dual image appliqué were sown many years ago when I was teaching a reverse appliqué workshop inspired by wrought iron grilles and grids. This workshop was initially for hand stitchers because that was what I could confidently teach, but as my machine sewing skills improved, I included a machine method in the workshop as well. During one such workshop, I casually suggested to those working by machine that they could discard or store the shapes that were cut away from the

fused, intact grid. After being challenged by a teacher attending the workshop that this was a waste of fabric, I set about there and then to find a way to use the cutouts. The answer was so obvious that by the end of the workshop I was demonstrating the solution to the students!

As I look back at the many quilts I have made, it has slowly dawned on me that the use of positive and negative shapes in design has been trying to surface in my work for a while. I taught general quiltmaking classes for years, putting my creative self on hold until half term and holiday breaks. Then I would pursue and develop projects that were specifically of interest to me, often in response to challenges.

POSITIVE PINK, NEGATIVE BLUE, 24" x 24"
The tile pattern is replicated
on either side of the diagonal.

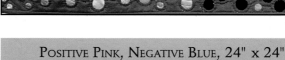

These early quilts were hand sewn, but curiosity led me to try a machine-made version of a hand-sewn quilt. I needed to know how the same rich colors looked on a cream background and machine appliqué seemed to be the quickest way to find out.

STRIPPY QUILTS REVISITED, 45" x 57"
The design is based on traditional strippy quilts, with quilting patterns used as stencils to provide the positive and negative effect.

SWIRLING SWALLOWS, Positive, 45" x 45"

SWIRLING SWALLOWS, Negative, 45" x 45"

ARCHED WINDOWS, Negative
41" x 54", hand reverse appliquéd

JACOBEAN FANTASY
Positive, detail

With growing confidence in my machine ability, I decided to revisit patterns based on Jacobean embroidery. Their complex shapes and intricate details became my personal challenge as a machine sewer.

ARCHED WINDOWS, Positive
41" x 54", machine appliquéd

I have been teaching dual image appliqué in the UK for several years
now, developing the book format as
my knowledge and confidence in the
method has increased. In its basic
form, seen in the heart Taster Block
(page 17) and the first three projects,
it is a simple and economical technique. But, as the later projects tes-
tify, it is also dynamic and extremely
versatile. So now the time has come
for you to try it for yourself, through
the pages of this book. Enjoy the fas-
cinating journey!

JACOBEAN FANTASY
Negative, detail

TERMINOLOGY: FRAME, FILLER, AND FOUNDATION

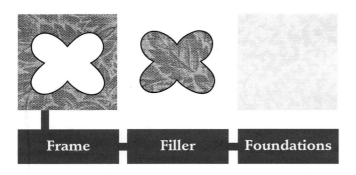

Frame   Filler   Foundations

WASTE NOT, WANT NOT, 18½" x 18½",
made by May Renee, Haslingden, Lancashire, UK

To make the instructions easier to follow, I use the following terminology:

The **Frame** (the negative image) is the intact, surrounding stencil shape that remains when the filler has been removed.

The **Filler** (the positive image) is the shape that is cut out and removed from the surrounding frame. This is marked with an X on the pattern and there could be any number of them.

The **Foundation** is the piece of fabric that goes behind the filler in a positive appliqué or behind the frame in a negative (reverse) appliqué.

DUAL IMAGE APPLIQUÉ IN A NUTSHELL

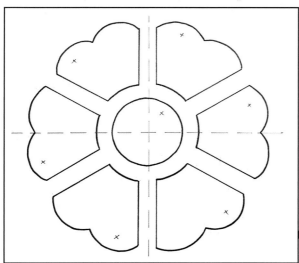

SELECTING A PATTERN

The pattern must look like a stencil so that the shapes, or fillers, can be removed, leaving an intact surround or frame.

Selecting a pattern

SELECTING THE FABRICS

Choose fabrics that contrast well. The frame and fillers are cut from a fabric that has had fusible web applied. Two foundations are needed, one to go behind the frame and the other to go behind the fillers.

CHRISTMAS PLACEMATS, 8" x 8",
made by Helen Bailey, Longridge, Lancashire, UK

PREPARING THE FUSIBLE

Enlarge and trace the pattern (page 83) onto the paper side of fusible web and cut out ½" beyond the marked line. Mark each filler with an X.

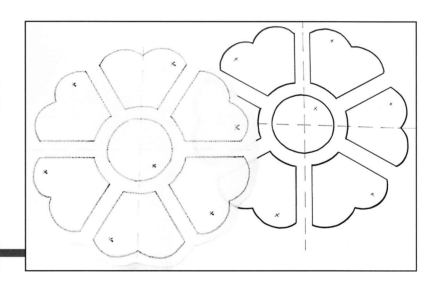

Preparing the fusible

IRONING THE FUSIBLE

Center the fused pattern and iron onto the wrong side of the frame/filler fabric.

Ironing the fusible

CUTTING AWAY THE FILLERS

Carefully cut away the marked fillers (shapes) exactly on the traced lines, leaving the frame intact.

Cutting away the fillers

MAKING THE POSITIVE APPLIQUÉ WITH THE FILLER

Use the frame, with its paper backing still on to position each filler, with its paper backing removed, onto the right side (RS) of a foundation fabric. Fuse the fillers in place and remove the frame. Place over cotton batting and sew along the cut edges of the fillers to secure them to the foundation, to prevent fraying, and to add texture.

Positive appliqué

MAKING THE NEGATIVE APPLIQUÉ WITH THE FRAME

Remove the paper backing from the frame and fuse it onto the RS of a foundation fabric. Cut away the excess fabric beyond the fused edges from the back. Place over cotton batting and sew along the cut edges of the frame to secure it to the foundation, to prevent fraying, and to add texture.

Negative appliqué

Note: Cotton batting is an essential part of the dual image technique. Placing it behind each block before the cut edges are sewn adds body to the shape and prevents distortion.

CHAPTER 2 ▶

Dual Image Appliqué
What Do I Need?

DUAL IMAGE APPLIQUÉ SUPPLIES

Supplies are a matter of personal choice, based on knowledge gained through experience. You only have to go to any quilting event to see that there is a bewildering array of supplies available to the modern quilter. The best I can do is tell you what you need specifically for dual image appliqué, to state my preferences where appropriate, and to explain why it works for me.

FUSIBLE WEB

Fusible web is a layer of adhesive attached to a protective paper backing. It is used to bond fabrics together quickly and accurately simply by ironing. A motif or pattern is traced onto the see-through backing, cut out, then ironed onto the wrong side (WS) of a fabric. The heat of the iron against the backing transfers the fusible onto the fabric. After the motif or pattern is cut out, the backing paper is removed so the motif can be fused onto a foundation fabric to secure it while the edges are stitched.

It is best to buy fusible on a roll and follow the manufacturer's instructions. I prefer Bondaweb®, as it's

known in the UK, or Wonder Under® brands. It is readily available and is cheaper and wider than the alternatives. The backing paper is easy to see through for tracing and becomes opaque when ironed, making it is easier to see when the adhesive has transferred. The adhesive is light and fibrous so the fabric does not become overly stiff and the paper is easy to remove.

MARKING TOOLS

Marking tools in the form of pencils, pens, felt tips, crayons, chalks, soapstone, and so on, are widely available. The aim is to find a suitable marker that remains visible for the length of time you are working with the fabric but also fades or is removable afterwards. Always test the marker on your fabric first, and follow the manufacturer's instructions.

For this method I use a chalk wheel to mark dark fabrics, a water erasable marker to mark light fabrics, and a fine pencil or a fine point permanent marker to trace the patterns onto the fusible backing paper.

Fusible web on a roll, for tracing, ironing, and transferring

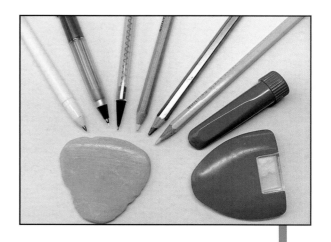

An array of markers

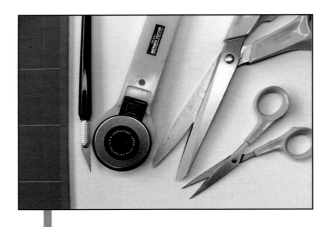

Cutting tools

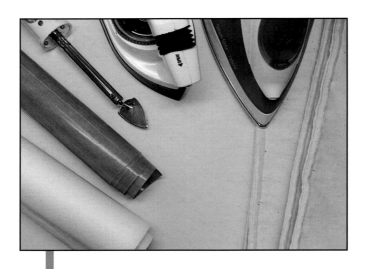

Irons, ironing surface, and protective sheets

A variety of suitable cotton fabrics

CUTTING TOOLS

Small sharp scissors that cut right to the point are essential for cutting the fillers from the frame. Use a rotary cutter, on a cutting mat, to cut right on the marked line of a fused-fabric filler shape to allow the point of the scissors into the shape. An X-Acto® or blade cutter is useful for cutting into small circles.

IRONS AND IRONING SURFACES

A large iron and ironing surface are essential for general pressing and thorough fusing. A smaller iron is useful for gently fusing the fillers while the positioning frame is in place. Use a non-stick or Teflon® pressing sheet, pressing paper, or baking parchment to protect the iron and ironing surface when using fusible web.

TIP: Much of the Dual Image Appliqué Method is based on ironing, so a larger than normal ironing surface is strongly recommended. You can make one easily by placing 2 layers of cotton batting between 2 layers of cotton fabric and sewing around the outside edge. Make it large enough for all the projects so you don't have to move the layers when fusing. You can use vertical pins to secure shapes before fusing. This surface is portable when attending workshops and easily stored.

FABRIC

Good quality cotton fabrics in a wide range of styles—from plains to prints and from stripes to painterly batiks—are recommended. There needs to be a good contrast between the frame/filler fabric and the foundation fabrics. I particularly like to use batiks because they are tightly woven and less likely to fray. Prewash the fabrics at your own discretion.

BATTING

A low-loft cotton batting grips the fabric during stitching, gives a lovely drape to completed wallhangings, and you can press it lightly with a warm iron. My personal favorite is Warm & Natural® Needled Cotton batting.

Cotton batting is essential.

RULERS

Choose rulers that are clear and uncomplicated, and that grip the fabric while you are cutting. Practice with them to become familiar with their markings. A circular template is useful for drawing perfect circles for cutting and sewing.

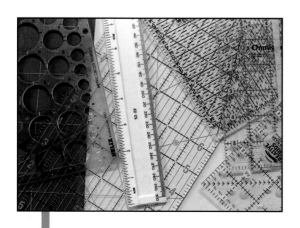

A variety of rulers

THREADS

Choice of threads comes down to personal preference and aesthetics. I prefer fine 50-weight 2 ply 100% cotton threads for appliqué, 40-weight rayon threads for free-motion quilting, and a heavier 30-weight cotton thread for straight-line quilting.

Threads for all occasions

SEWING MACHINE

Apart from a modest range of straight and swing or zig-zag stitches, these are the sewing machine functions I would recommend you should look for when choosing a new machine:

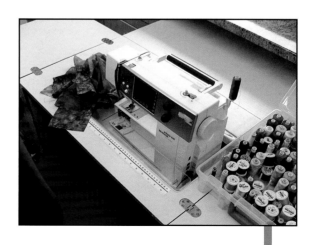

Sewing station

a. **Manual stitch controls** for both straight and zigzag stitches that allow you to increase and decrease the stitch length and width smoothly and evenly while the machine is sewing.

b. **A needle-down function** so that when you stop stitching, the needle position is down in the fabric, holding it firmly so you can reposition your hands for sewing the next section.

c. **A sensitive foot pedal** that stops the machine sewing immediately when you lift your foot off the pedal and doesn't run on for a couple more stitches.

d. **A speed control switch** that adjusts the speed of the stitching to allow fast sewing on straight edges or slower, more controlled sewing on more complex shapes.

e. **A knee lift** that lifts and lowers the machine foot, thus freeing your hands to control and adjust your project.

f. **Feed dogs** that drop or can be covered so they do not inhibit free-motion quilting.

g. **A generous flat area stitching platform** for good visibility and support around the needle.

h. **A stable, adjustable chair** with height control and a back that tilts helps avoid strain on your back and shoulders.

SEWING MACHINE ACCESSORIES

a. **A walking foot,** also known as an even-feed foot, has its own feed dogs that work with those of the machine to grab all the fabric layers and feed them together and evenly under the needle during sewing. It is useful when stitching the straight lines or gentle curves of a layered quilt.

b. **The quarter-inch foot** helps you sew an accurate and consistent ¼" seam allowance.

c. **An open-toe appliqué foot** has no metal in front of the needle, allowing excellent visibility. There should be a wide groove underneath to allow the ridge of stitching to move freely under the foot.

d. **A darning or free-motion foot** goes up with the needle to create space to maneuver the project freely and then lowers with the needle to hold the fabric down on the sewing plate to sew the stitch. Choose one that enables you to see the design around the needle easily.

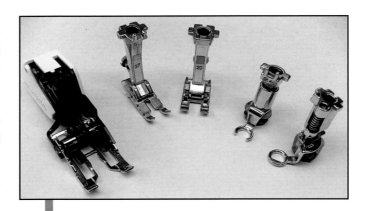

Machine feet   Needles

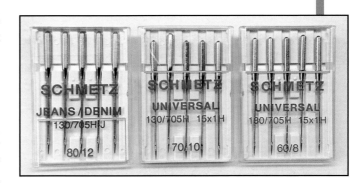

e. **Good quality needles** that suit your sewing thread are important. A lower number indicates a finer needle. I use a fine 60/8 needle with the fine 50-weight threads; a 70/10 needle with 40-weight rayon threads; and an 80/12 with heavier 30-weight cotton threads.

CHAPTER 3 ▶ Dual Image Appliqué How Do I Do It? Taster Block

TERMINOLOGY – FRAME FILLER FOUNDATIONS

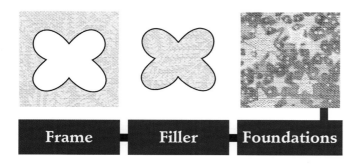

| Frame | Filler | Foundations |

One pattern produces two blocks, so nothing is wasted. The filler is removed from the frame and fused onto a foundation fabric to make a positive appliqué. The remaining frame is fused onto a foundation fabric to make a reverse or negative appliqué. A batting layer is added before sewing so the appliqué stitch is also the quilting stitch.

RS = right side   WS = wrong side

DUAL IMAGE APPLIQUÉ

The instructions for preparing dual image machine appliqué are illustrated with the heart motif but they are applicable to all the patterns.

PREPARE THE FUSIBLE

Enlarge and trace pattern (page 83) and centering lines onto the paper side of the fusible. Mark the center point. Mark the filler (the heart motif) with an X. Trim away the extra fusible web to measure ½" beyond the outer edges of the marked pattern.

TIP: Get into the habit of marking all the fillers with an X. This helps you to identify which pieces you are cutting away on more complex patterns.

TIP: Extra fusible web extending more than ½" beyond the edges of the marked pattern is wasteful and makes the fabric stiff and unyielding.

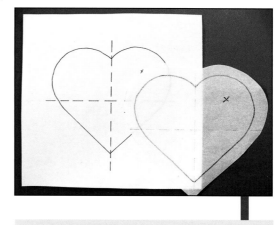

Preparing the fusible

IRON THE FUSIBLE

Find the center of the appliqué fabric by gently folding it in quarters and finger-pressing the center folds. Place the fabric WS up on an ironing board. Center the fusible web on top with paper-side up. Press carefully and let it cool.

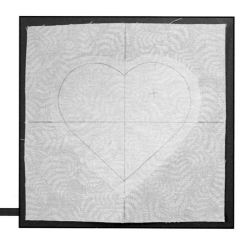

Ironing the fusible

DUAL IMAGE APPLIQUÉ BY DILYS FRONKS **17**

Cutting out the filler

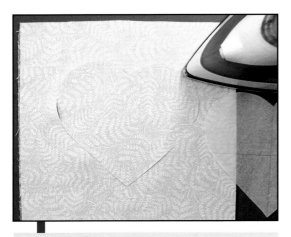

Using the frame to position the filler

Removing the frame

TIP: The fusing process is virtually impossible to undo so remember that you only have one attempt to get this right! When fusing larger pieces of fabric, get in the habit of pressing from the center to the edges. Take extra care to make sure that the outer edge is well fused.

CUT OUT THE FILLER

Place the fused square, RS down, onto a cutting board so that the pattern lines are uppermost. Use a rotary-cutter blade to make a clean incision right on the line. Use small sharp scissors to carefully cut out and remove the filler from the frame. Do not remove the paper until you are ready to use the pieces.

MAKE THE POSITIVE APPLIQUÉ WITH THE FILLER

Place a square of foundation fabric, RS up, on an ironing surface. Place the frame, with its backing paper still on, RS up, on top so that the outer edges are matching. Remove the paper backing from the filler and place it back inside the frame. Use the toe of the iron to gently stick the filler in place.

Remove the frame and iron the filler with a lift and press method to fuse it thoroughly.

TIP: Always use a lift and press method of fusing. Dragging the iron can distort and shift the fabrics and lift the corners of more complex shapes.

MAKE THE NEGATIVE APPLIQUÉ WITH THE FRAME

Place a square of foundation fabric, RS up, on the ironing surface. Remove the paper backing from the frame and place it RS up on top so that the outer edges are matching. Use the iron to fuse the frame in place.

From the WS, trim away the excess foundation fabric that lies beyond the fused edges.

TIP: The excess background fabric can be folded and creased on straight edges, ready for cutting with scissors used flat against the fabric. For cutting more intricate shapes, a light box is invaluable.

Place and pin the prepared appliqués onto the batting square ready for sewing.

PREPARE A PRACTICE SEWING SAMPLE

Let's try a simple pattern to help you understand the mechanics of machine appliqué. On the positive appliqué, made with the filler, sew round the outside edge of the heart. On the negative appliqué, made with the frame, sew round the inside edge of the frame.

TIP: The nature of the cut edges becomes reversed for each sample. An outward point and convex curves on the positive sample becomes an inward point and concave curves on the negative sample.

Both the mouse and heart motifs have all the shapes you'll need to sew when you come to do the projects—namely concave and convex curves; outward corners and points; inward corners and V's; straight and curved lines.

The instructions are specific to the mouse motif, but you can choose to do the heart instead. This is a practical step-by-step guide to machine appliqué that applies to all the projects.

It is important to have the right mindset when trying something new or repeating something you believe you are not good at. You are the only one who is going to judge this sample, so be relaxed and open-minded!

REQUIREMENTS

    Frame and filler: 4½" x 4½" square of light fabric
    Foundation and backing: 2 squares 9" x 9"
    Batting: 9" x 9" square
    Fusible web: 4" x 4" square

On a 9" foundation fabric square, use a pencil to trace the mouse motif and a ruler to draw 6 lines.

Enlarge the mouse pattern (page 83). Use a pencil to trace the mouse motif onto the center of the paper side of the square of fusible web. Iron the fusible onto the WS of the square of appliqué fabric (the frame/filler fabric).

Cut the motif out on the line to produce both frame and filler. Fuse each piece to a square of foundation fabric as shown. Place onto the batting and backing square. Pin baste with safety pins to hold the layers together.

Pin baste with safety pins.

Place the frame onto the foundation.

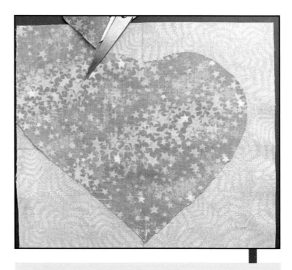

Trim away the excess foundation fabric from the back.

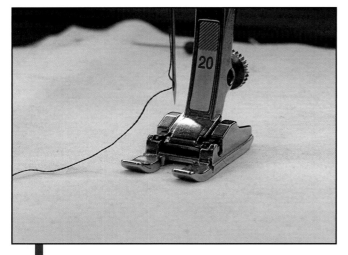

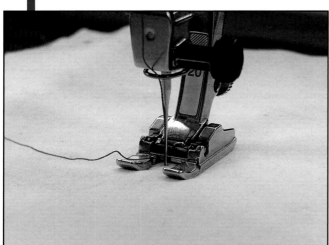

Bring the bobbin thread to the top.

PREPARING TO SEW

TIP: As a new quilter, I bought my first sewing machine about 26 years ago and I was grateful to discover that it had a tortoise and hare switch. If I used the tortoise setting, it didn't matter how heavy-footed I was on the pedal; the machine just slowly and deliberately chugged along giving me the feeling I was in control. The hare setting, in comparison, seemed like freeway driving! If you are inexperienced on your machine and you are able to control the speed of the stitch, start slowly and build up your speed as you become more confident.

Choose a suitable thread that shows up well against your chosen fabrics. Prepare the bobbin and thread the machine. Fit a new needle and an open-toe appliqué foot, check your sewing position, and make sure the light is good.

TIP: The thread for machine appliqué can match the fabric to blend into the edge of the shape, or it can contrast with the fabric to define the edge more strongly. For this exercise, use a contrasting thread so that you can see your stitches and continually assess your progress.

STARTING TO SEW

EXERCISE A: BRINGING THE BOBBIN THREAD TO THE TOP

Set the machine to sew a straight stitch. To prevent tangled threads on the back of a project, get into the habit of doing the following simple maneuver at the start of a machine-sewn line.

Line up the needle where you want to start. Hold the thread loosely and lower the presser foot onto the fabric.

Hold onto the top thread, without adding tension, and sew a single stitch.

Lift the foot and slightly pull the fabric toward yourself. Tug on the top thread to pull the bobbin thread onto the top of the work.

Reposition the fabric under the foot and ease the needle back into the same hole. Put the presser foot down again, ready for sewing. Practice this several times to get used to it.

EXERCISE B: SIGNING ON AND SIGNING OFF

Line 1: To start, or "sign on," adjust the straight stitch length so you get about six tiny stitches in ¼" and sew them at the start of a marked line. Go back to a normal straight stitch setting and sew along the rest of the line, stopping ¼" from the end. Return to the tiny stitches and sew six more to finish or "sign off."

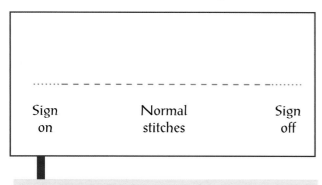

| Sign on | Normal stitches | Sign off |

Sign on, normal stitches, sign off

TIP: Some sewing machines have a lock stitch for starting and finishing. Test to see that this process doesn't leave an obvious and unsightly mound of thread on the fabric. If you are happy with the way it looks, use it.

EXERCISE C: UNDERSTANDING THE ZIGZAG STITCH

The purpose of the zigzag stitch is to cover the cut edges of the appliqué, to stabilize them, and prevent them from fraying. In dual image appliqué, the cut edges are fused so a very close zigzag stitch, or satin stitch, is not entirely necessary.

Line 2: Sign on at the start of line 2 and, with the needle out of the fabric, set the machine to sew a zigzag stitch. Without any adjustment in the position of needle or fabric, sew a line of zigzag stitches along a marked line and sign off. Look at the stitches to register that they swing the same distance on each side of the marked line.

TIP: The "zig" part of my stitch swings to my left and the "zag" part to my right as I am facing my machine. I always sew clockwise around the edges of the fillers (positive) and counterclockwise around the frames (negative). In other words, my appliqué shape is always to the left of the needle and the foundation fabric is always on the right.

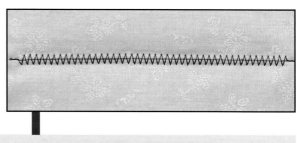

Stitches swing the same distance on either side of center.

EXERCISE D: ADJUSTING THE ZIGZAG STITCH

Line 3: To explore the width of the zigzag stitches, sign on at the start of line 3 and sew some zigzag stitches using different width control settings on your machine.

If the zigzag stitch dial number is low, the zigzag is narrow.
If the zigzag stitch dial number is high, the zigzag is wide.

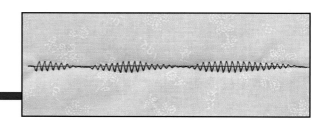

Zigzag with different width settings

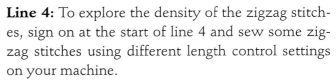

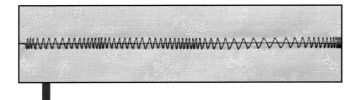

Zigzag with different length settings

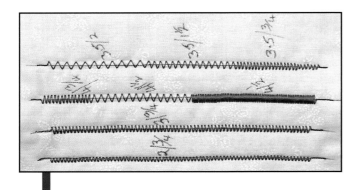

Record different settings and their stitches.

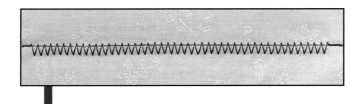

Use your chosen setting to
sew to one side of the line.

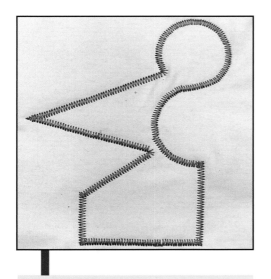

Sew around the traced
mouse motif.

Line 4: To explore the density of the zigzag stitches, sign on at the start of line 4 and sew some zigzag stitches using different length control settings on your machine.

If the straight stitch dial number is low, the stitches are close together. If the straight stitch dial number is high, the stitches are farther apart.

It is a combination and balance of these two settings that give the width and density of the zigzag stitch you require. I generally work with the straight stitch set at ¾ and the width stitch at 2, but machines vary. Find a stitch that suits you.

Line 5: Use this line, and the space between the lines if necessary, to try out a combination of width and length settings. Use a permanent marker to write the settings beside the stitches to help you to decide which combination you would like to use.

TIP: Write your chosen settings on masking tape and stick it onto your machine, so you don't forget them during breaks from sewing. If you have a computerized machine, enter the information into the memory for instant recall.

Line 6: In dual image appliqué, most of the stitch should lie on the cut edge of the frame or filler, with the outward swing of the stitch entering the foundation fabric right at the cut edge.

Imagine this line is the edge of an appliqué shape. Sign on, set the zigzag stitch to your chosen settings, and adjust the fabric in relation to the needle, so that most of the stitch lies to one side of the line. Stitch along the line and sign off.

TIP: Most modern machines allow you to change the position of your needle. If you are familiar with the function, use it to adjust the needle to the fabric rather than the fabric to the needle.

EXERCISE E: SEWING AROUND THE TRACED MOUSE MOTIF

Although it is blindingly obvious to say, it is worth pointing out that the machine is designed to sew in a straight line. The presser foot goes down to hold the fabric on the sewing plate, where the teeth move with each stitch to ease the fabric away from the sewer. It is you, the sewer, who has to guide the fabric and make adjustments so that the machine can change direction.

TIP: It is helpful if the needle stays down in the fabric every time you stop sewing to anchor it while the fabric is adjusted. If you have a needle down feature on your machine, use it.

Start to sew on the traced mouse motif first so that the quality of your stitches can be clearly monitored and your progress easily assessed. Treat it as an appliqué shape and sew with the motif on the left-hand side of the needle. Work in a controlled way to sew clockwise around the shape as follows.

Sign on directly on the marked line, then take the needle out of the fabric to adjust the controls to your chosen zigzag setting. Put the needle back into the fabric at the end of the tiny stitches so that the first stitch swings to the left (zig). Sew along the shape until you reach the corner.

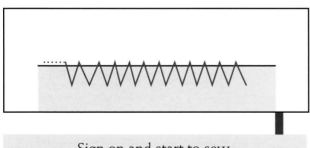

Sign on and start to sew.

The outward corner: Sew to just beyond the corner, stopping after the zag swing, with the needle down at the dot on the foundation fabric (a). Note that the following zig is going to swing to the left. Pivot on the dot to rotate the shape 90 degrees so that the zig stitch

swings on top of the stitches that have just been sewn (b). Continue sewing away from the corner.

TIP: To pivot, stop with the needle down in the fabric, raise the presser foot, and reposition the fabric. You can pivot on either side of the stitch.

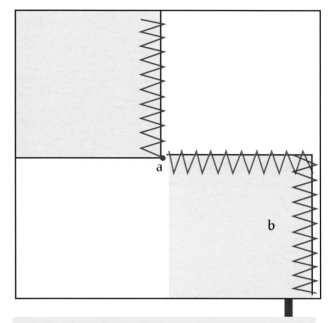

Pivot 90 degrees at dot on outward corner.

The elongated point: When sewing a sharp point, the needle eventually starts to swing into the foundation fabric on both sides of the appliqué shape. Stop with the needle down at the dot (a, page 24) to adjust the fabric slightly so that the point lies centrally under the foot. Continue to sew slowly toward the end, reducing the width of the swing until there is no sideways movement at all.

Leave the needle in the fabric and pivot at the dot (b) to rotate the fabric 180 degrees. As you start to sew again, gradually increase the width of the swing back to your chosen setting (c), pivot slightly and continue to sew away from the point.

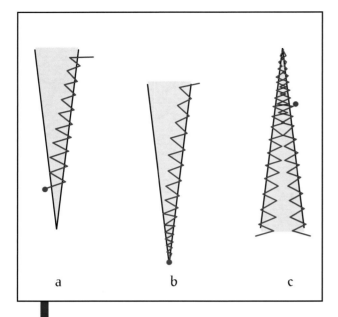

Pivot slightly at a and c; rotate 180 degrees at b on an elongated point.

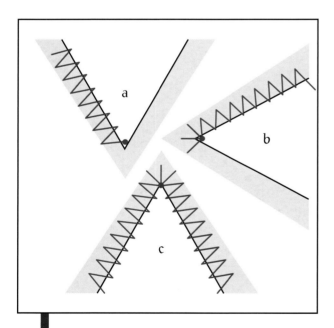

Pivot at the dot for 3 stitches into an inward V.

Pivot in the foundation fabric at regular intervals on a convex curve.

The inward V: Stop sewing when the needle is at the dot in the V (a), with the needle down in the foundation fabric. Sew three separate and complete zigzag stitches into the V, holding onto the fabric so that that there is no forward movement. Do one stitch just before the V, one right on the V and one just after (b), making sure that each zag goes into the same hole at the dot to get around the shape. Pivot and continue sewing along the next edge.

The curves: When sewing a curved edge, keep in mind that the zigzag stitch has an inside and outside edge. Adjustments are always made on the side of the stitch that has to travel the longest distance, with the general rule that the tighter the curve, the more the stitch needs to be adjusted.

TIP: On gentle curves, the hands can ease the fabric under the needle during sewing, so the direction of the stitch follows the curve. The sewing needs to be done slowly, with gentle guidance so that the fabric layers don't distort.

The convex curve: The right side of the stitch on a convex curve has to travel a longer distance than the left side so all adjustments are made with the needle down in the foundation fabric, after the zag swing. Lift the presser foot and pivot the fabric slightly to alter the sewing direction. If adjustments are made on the other side of the stitch, gaps will be left around the edge.

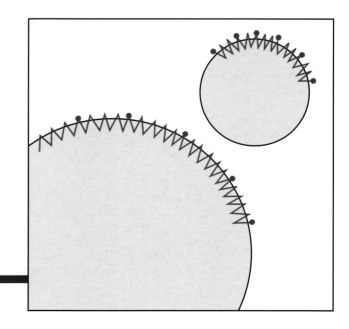

The concave curve: The left side of the stitch on a concave curve has to travel a longer distance so all adjustments are made with the needle down in the appliquéd shape, after the zig swing. If adjustments are made on the other side of the stitch, gaps will be left around the edge.

Finishing: When you get back to where you started, zigzag over the sign on stitches to cover them. When the zigzag stitches meet, adjust the machine to sew tiny straight stitches again. Reposition the fabric so that the needle sews along one side or the other of the zigzag stitches, wherever they will be best concealed. Sign off with a few tiny stitches to complete.

EXERCISE F: SEWING THE FUSED SHAPES

The fused filler is the same shape as the traced motif in the exercise above, so repeat the clockwise stitching sequence around the outside of the fabric shape.

Check the position of the stitches along the fused edge. If they are inside the cut edges (a), the threads can separate, resulting in a frayed look. If they are well outside the cut edges, the shape can pull away from the stitches.

Sew counterclockwise around the inside edge of the frame for further practice. You will note that the curves and points of the frame are the opposite to those of the filler.

The more you practice these exercises, the better acquainted you will become with your sewing machine. Work with it to get to know it well and it will become a reliable and creative friend!

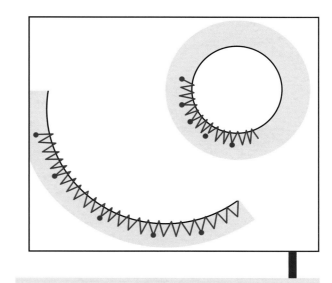

Pivot in the appliqué fabric at regular intervals on the concave curves.

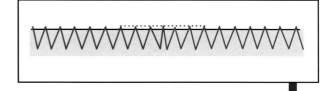

Complete the shape and sign off.

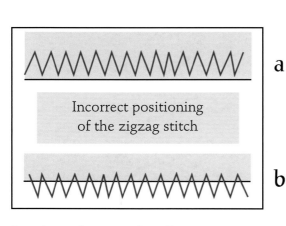

Incorrect positioning
of the zigzag stitch

a

b

Sew around the fused filler.

Sew around the fused frame.

With the fillers

With the frames

With the frames

With the fillers

Mosaic Flowers Tote Bags, 17" x 17", front and back, made by the author

CHAPTER 4 ▶

MOSAIC FLOWERS TOTE BAGS

FLOWER WREATH BAG, 16" x 16", made by
Ruth Wallett, Clipston, Northamptonshire, UK

MOSAIC FLOWER TOTE BAGS, 18" x 18", made by
Judith D. Ayton, Green Norton, Northamptonshire, UK

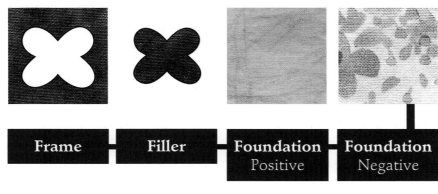

Frame	Filler	Foundation Positive	Foundation Negative

You can never have enough bags! You need bags to match your outfits and bags to carry your supplies to class. Bags can conceal all the fabric you buy to keep the stash overflowing, and they can be decoratively useful for storing a quilt. They make wonderful gifts or even warm and cozy cat beds!

The instructions are for two bags using both patterns (page 84). The frames are used to make one bag and the fillers are used to make the other.

Review Chapter 3 for detailed Dual Image Appliqué instructions.

REQUIREMENTS FOR BOTH BAGS

Frames, fillers, and handles:
   1 yard of dark fabric
Foundations, linings, bindings, and handles:
   1¼ yards each of 2 contrasting fabrics, one floral and one plain (2½ yards total)
Batting:
   4 squares 20" x 20" for bag sides and 4 strips 26" x 1¼" for handles
Fusible web:
   2 squares 14" x 14"
Machine threads:
   To match the fabrics

CUTTING

Dark fabric:
   2 squares 18" x 18" for the fillers/frames
   1 strip 2" x 40" for binding the top
   8 strips 26" x 1¾" for the handles

Cut out the fillers accurately and keep them in sequence to save time later when repositioning them.

Place the frame onto the foundation and replace the fillers.

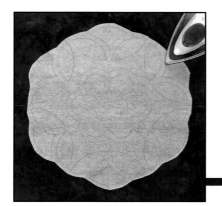

Iron the fusible onto the WS of the fabric.

Contrasting floral fabric:
  2 squares 14" x 14" for the foundations behind the frames
  2 squares 20" x 20" for backing (the bag lining)
  2 strips 1¼" x 26" for the handles
  2 straight-cut strips 1¼" x 40" for binding the inside seam
  1 straight-cut strip 2" x 40" for binding the top
  Optional: 1 strip 2" x 18" for safety strap

Contrasting plain fabric:
  2 squares 18" x 18" for the foundations behind the fillers
  2 squares 20" x 20" for lining
  2 strips 1¼" x 26" for the handles
  2 straight-cut strips 1¼" x 40" for binding the inside seam
  Optional: 1 strip 2" x 18" for safety strap

Follow these instructions for both patterns.

PREPARING THE FUSIBLE

Enlarge and trace both patterns (page 84) onto the fusible web and trim away the excess fusible, leaving ½" beyond the outer marked line. Fuse to the WS of the dark fabric squares. Allow them to cool.

Cut out the fillers. Keep them in sequence.

TIP: Mark the paper on the frame to show where you start from, and number the shapes clockwise to help with their placement.

CONSTRUCTING THE PANELS

Check to make sure you know where the marked numbering sequence begins on the frame. With its backing paper still on, center the frame, RS up, onto the RS of an 18" square of plain foundation fabric. Remove the paper backing from the fillers and place them back into position within the frame.

Fuse the fillers onto a foundation.

Fuse the frame onto a foundation.

Trim away the excess fabric from the back.

TIP: Be aware that the marked numbering sequence now goes counterclockwise.

Use the tip of the iron to gently fuse the fillers onto the foundation. Remove the frame and fuse them thoroughly to complete the positive block.

Remove the paper backing from the frame and fuse it onto a 14" square of patterned foundation fabric.

From the back, carefully trim away the excess fabric beyond the fused edge to complete the negative block.

Repeat these steps with the second pattern.

Completed panels

Layer and pin baste each panel with batting and backing, matching the raw edges of the backing fabric with those on the front. Use matching thread and a small zigzag stitch to sew around the cut edges, working away from the center.

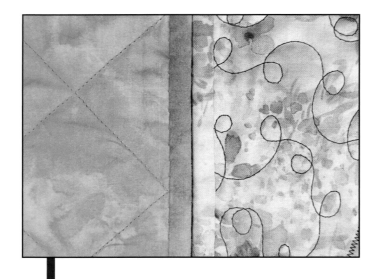

Appliqué and quilt the blocks.

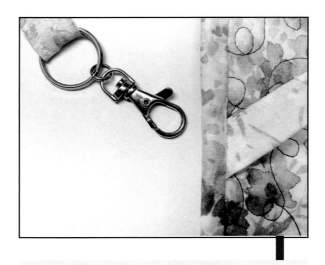

Optional security strap

Quilt the remaining areas outside the design to your satisfaction. One bag was quilted with a 2" diagonal grid and the other was free-motion quilted.

Trim the 4 panels to measure 17" x 17".

CONSTRUCTING THE BAGS

For the optional security strap, fold over ¼" on the long edges of the 2" x 18" strip and press. Fold one end ¼" and press. Fold in half lengthwise, WS together, and topstitch.

Place at an angle, pointing toward what will be the bottom of the bag, about 3" down from the top and baste in place.

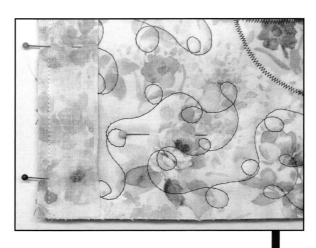

Sew and bind the panels.

Join the 1¼" x 40" binding strips to make a 56" length. With raw edges even and RS together, pin 2 quilted panels together. Sew the binding strip around 3 sides, mitering the corners. Trim the strip even with the top of the panels, turn under, and finish by hand.

Shape the bag at the base by sewing across the corner, 1½" from the tip. Fold the tip down toward the seam on the base of the bag and secure it by hand.

Fold the 2" x 40" binding strip in half lengthwise, WS together, and press. Sew along the outside top edge of the bag with a ¼" seam. Fold to the inside and finish by hand.

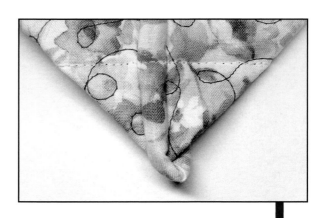

Shape the base of the bag.

CONSTRUCTING THE HANDLES

Pin the 1¼" x 26" strips of contrasting fabric, RS up, onto the 1¼" x 26" strips of batting.

With RS together, sew a 1¼" x 26" dark strip along the length of the batting strip with a ¼" seam. Iron the dark strip onto the back of the batting, leaving ¼" showing on the right side. Attach a second dark strip to the other side as shown.

Turn under and pin the raw edge so that the fold lies centrally along the length.

TIP: Secure with pins at right angles to the seam so they can be easily removed during sewing.

Working from the RS, use the dark thread to sew a line of decorative stitches down the middle of the handle to secure the seam on the back. Trim to measure 24".

To attach the handles, find the center of the top edge of each side. Measure 2½" from the center point of each side and mark it with a pin. Fold under the raw edge of the handle and place it on the outside edge of the marker pin. Sew through all the layers to secure it to the outside of the bag. Sew the other end of the handle on the outside edge of the other marker pin to complete.

Repeat these steps for the 4 handles for the 2 bags.

Attach the dark strips to the handle fabric and batting.

The back of the handles

Sew down the middle of the strap with a decorative stitch.

Sew the handles in place.

CAT IN THE WINDOW WALLHANGING AND PILLOW

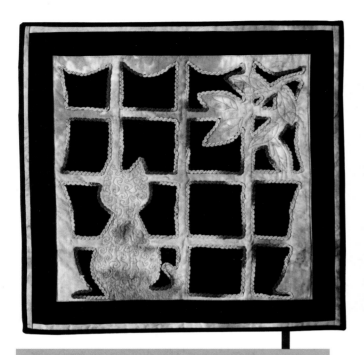

CAT IN THE WINDOW PILLOW, 18" x 18", made by the author. A light box was used to position the filler pieces, which were covered with a decorative cord during the appliqué. A contrasting strip is inserted when applying the binding.

CAT IN THE WINDOW WALLHANGING, 18" x 18", made by the author. The foundation was quilted prior to appliquéing the frame.

Use these simple but striking silhouettes to make a pair of complementary pillows or a pillow and wallhanging to display together.

Review Chapter 3 for detailed Dual Image Appliqué instructions.

REQUIREMENTS

Yardage is given for both the wallhanging and pillow.

Frame, fillers, borders, backings, bindings, and hanging sleeve: 1¾ yards of black fabric

Foundations and binding inserts: ½ yard of contrasting fabric

Fusible web: 1 square 13" x 13"

Batting for appliqué and quilting: 2 squares 21" x 21" (cotton batting allows gentle ironing)

Machine thread: black

Decorative cord: 6 yards

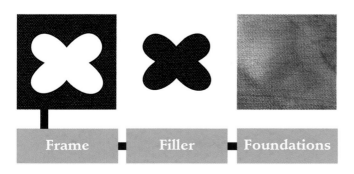

Frame · Filler · Foundations

CUTTING

Black fabric:
   1 square 18½" x 18½" for frame and fillers
   1 square 21" x 21" for the wallhanging backing
   1 strip 18" x 4½" for the hanging sleeve
   1 rectangle 10" x 18" and 1 rectangle 14" x 18" for
      the overlapped pillow back
   2 strips 2½" x 15" and 2 strips 2½" x 19" for the
      pillow borders
   4 strips 2" wide for the straight-of-grain binding
Contrasting fabric:
   2 squares 15" x 15" for the foundations
   8 strips 1" x 18" for binding inserts

PREPARING THE FUSIBLE

Enlarge and trace the pattern (page 85) onto the fusible web and trim away the excess fusible, leaving ½" beyond the outer marked line. Fuse to the WS of the black fabric. Allow it to cool.

Cut out the fillers. Keep them in sequence.

CONSTRUCTING THE PILLOW

Sew the 2½" black border strips to the 15" x 15" foundation square. Use a light box to center the fabric, RS up, onto the reverse side of the pattern. Pin to hold the layers together. Remove the backing papers from the fillers and lightly fuse them in place. Press on an ironing surface to fuse them thoroughly.

Layer the pillow front with batting and backing. Appliqué the fillers by couching decorative cord around the edges with matching thread and a zigzag stitch. Quilt the remaining areas to your satisfaction.

Trim the pillow top to measure 18" x 18". Fold the 1" strips of contrasting fabric in half lengthwise and press. Baste them around the edge of the pillow with a ⅛" seam.

Iron the fusible onto
the WS of the fabric.

Add black borders and
fuse the fillers.

Appliqué with couched
decorative cord and quilting to
add detail and texture.

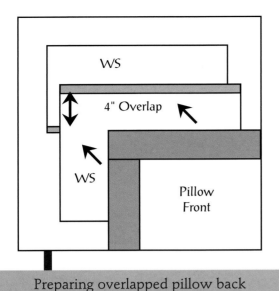

Preparing overlapped pillow back

Fold under one long edge of both pillow backing pieces ¼", then ¼" again. Stitch in place with a zigzag stitch. Layer with the pillow top, WS together, matching the raw edges.

Join 2 binding strips end-to-end, fold in half lengthwise, and add to the front with a ¼" seam, sewing through all thicknesses. Fold to the back and hand finish.

CONSTRUCTING THE WALLHANGING

Center a 15" x 15" square of foundation fabric, RS up, over the pattern and pin to secure them together. Place on a light box (or against a window) and use a suitable marker to draw a line around the edge of the pattern, about 1" beyond the outer marked lines.

Layer with the batting and backing squares and pin baste. Add free-motion machine quilting within the marked line with matching threads.

TIP: By choosing threads that match the colors within the fabric, the stitches will only add texture and blend into the background rather than show as an obvious design. Just relax and have fun with your machine!

The batting sandwich becomes slightly smaller during quilting, so check to see that the quilted area extends beyond the edges of the frame. Trim away the unquilted contrasting fabric only, ½" beyond the quilted edge.

Remove the backing paper from the frame and center it, RS up, on top of the quilted foundation square. Cover it with a Teflon sheet or a layer of baking parchment and fuse the frame onto the quilted foundation.

Appliqué the edges through all the layers using a stitch of your choice. The sample was sewn with a free-motion straight stitch, with a wavy line around the edges of the leaves.

Trim the appliquéd wallhanging to measure 18" x 18". Fold 1" strips of contrasting fabric in half lengthwise and press. Baste them in place around the edge of the wallhanging with a ⅛" seam. Make a sleeve (page 79) and bind to complete.

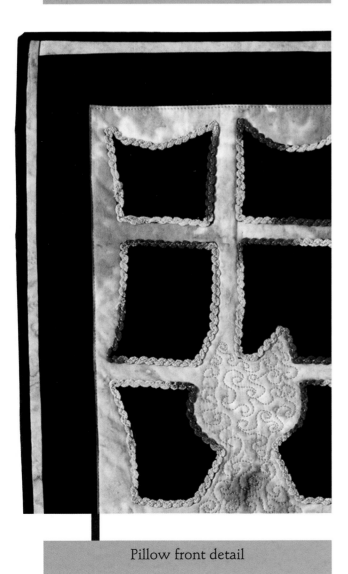

Pillow front detail

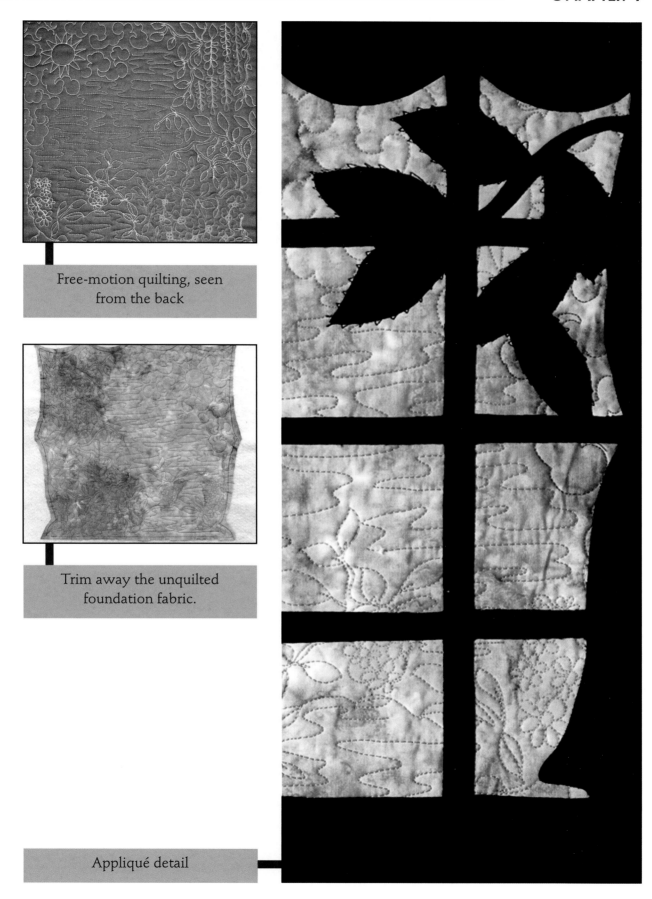

Free-motion quilting, seen from the back

Trim away the unquilted foundation fabric.

Appliqué detail

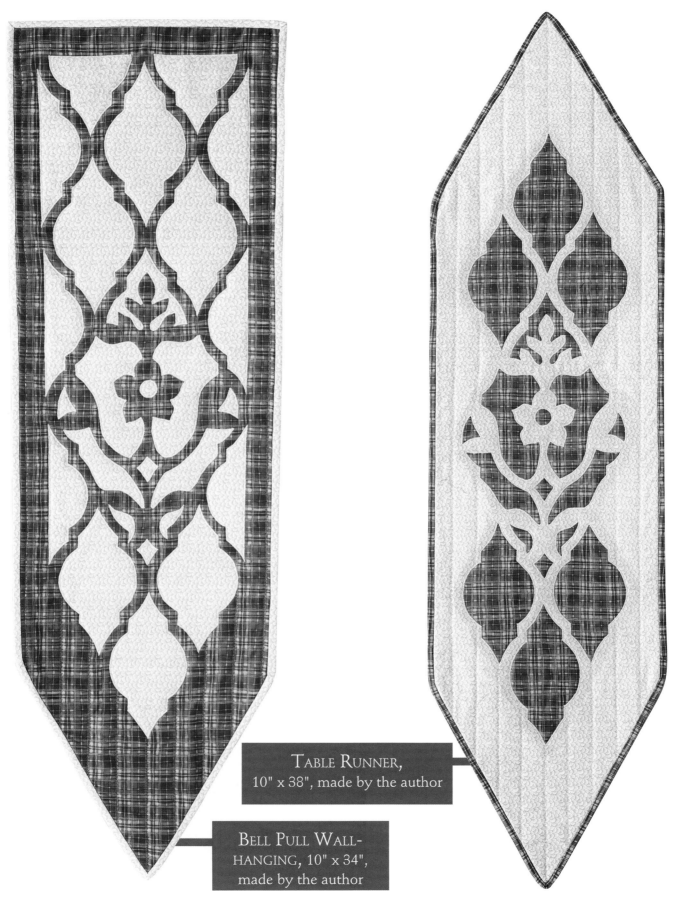

TABLE RUNNER,
10" x 38", made by the author

BELL PULL WALL-
HANGING, 10" x 34",
made by the author

BELL PULL WALLHANGING AND TABLE RUNNER

The wallhanging and table runner make a decorative and colorful addition to any home, especially if they are made to match the décor of a room. Long, thin wallhangings are reminiscent of the old bell pulls and are easy to hang beside a fireplace, in an alcove, or alongside a door. The shape is also suitable for a table runner as the length can be altered to suit your table.

This project uses a light fabric for the frame and fillers and shows you how to prepare extra fillers to extend the pattern. The length necessitates careful handling and maneuvering during sewing.

Review Chapter 3 for detailed Dual Image Appliqué instructions.

REQUIREMENTS

Frame, fillers, and binding: ¾ yard of light fabric
Foundations: ¾ yard of contrasting medium fabric
Batting for appliqué and quilting: 2 strips 12" x 40" (matches backing)
Backing: ¾ yard
Fusible: 1 strip 9"x 30" and 1 square 8" x 8" for additional shapes
Machine threads: to match both fabrics

CUTTING

Light fabric:
   1 strip 11" x 40" for the frame and fillers
   3 strips 2" wide for binding the bell pull
Contrasting fabric:
   2 strips 11" x 40" (as light fabric) for the foundations
   3 strips 2" wide for binding the table runner
Backing:
   2 rectangles 12" x 42"
   1 strip 4½" x 10" for the bell pull sleeve

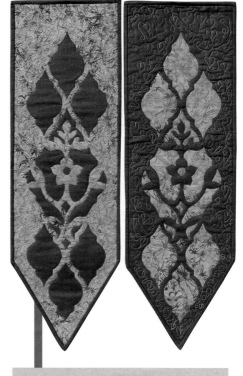

TWO FOR THE PRICE OF ONE, 10" x 32", made by Pauline Brown, Oswestry, Knockin Heath, Shropshire, UK

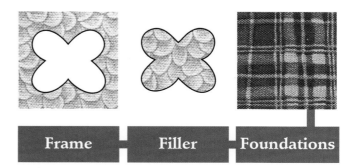

| Frame | Filler | Foundations |

PREPARING THE FUSIBLE

Enlarge and trace the pattern (page 86) onto the fusible web and trim away the excess fusible, leaving a ½" beyond the outer marked line. Fuse to the WS of the filler/frame fabric. Allow it to cool.

Cut out the fillers. Keep them in sequence.

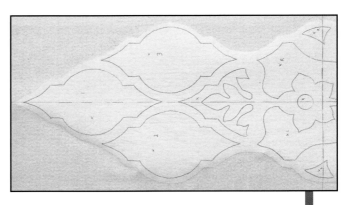

Iron the fusible onto the WS of the light filler/frame fabric.

Cut out the fillers accurately and keep them in sequence.

AUDITIONING FOUNDATION FABRICS

The dual image technique allows you to audition several foundation fabrics before you make a final choice. Pin a fabric behind the frame, hang it up, and go to the other side of the room to see how it looks. You'll know when the combination is right for you.

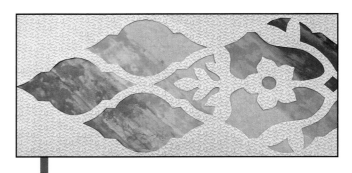

Audition a bright fabric. A bit overpowering perhaps?

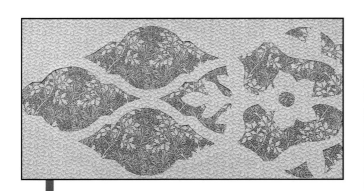

Audition a light fabric. Not much contrast.

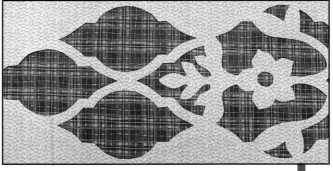

Audition a medium fabric. Just right!

CONSTRUCTING THE PANELS

Place the frame, with backing paper still on, RS up, onto the RS of the foundation, aligning the edges.

Remove the backing paper from the fillers and place them in position within the frame. Use the tip of the iron to gently fuse the fillers in place. Remove the frame and fuse the fillers onto the foundation thoroughly to complete the positive block.

Remove the paper backing from the frame and fuse it onto the remaining 11" x 40" strip of foundation fabric. Trim away the excess foundation fabric beyond the fused edge.

Trace 4 tile shapes from the pattern onto the paper side of the fusible and iron them onto the WS of the light fabric. Draw a line from point to point to divide 3 of the shapes in half vertically and 1 in half horizontally.

Cut the additional fillers out on the marked lines. Use the pattern and a light box to position them accurately before fusing them thoroughly.

QUILTING THE PANELS

TIP: If you are using a stripy fabric, quilt along selected lines of the pattern.

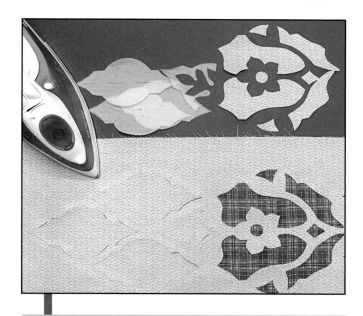

Position the frame on the foundation and replace the fillers.

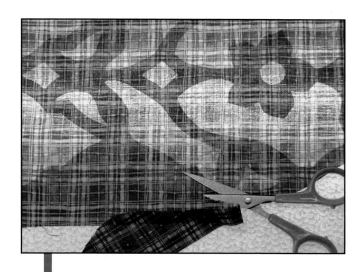

Use a light box to trim away the excess fabric.

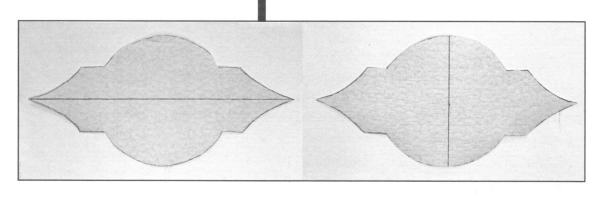

Marking the additional tile shapes

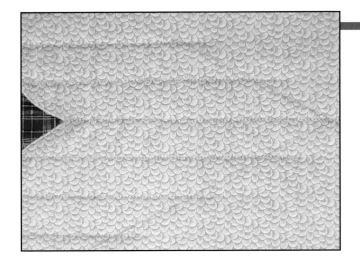

the two panel images on the left

Use a light box to position
the additional fillers accurately.

Marking the tapered end

To define the tapered ends (2 on the frame/table runner and 1 on the filler/bell pull), put a mark 6" from the point of the ending appliqué shape. Put a ruler on this mark and adjust it so that the 3" line rests against the edge of the outside appliqué shape. Mark along the edge of the ruler and repeat for the other side.

Use a suitable marker to draw quilting lines at 1" intervals, starting at the center point and working outwards.

Pin baste each panel with the batting and backing. Use matching thread and a small zigzag to sew around the cut edges, working from the center.

Quilt along the marked lines with small herring-bone stitches from the appliqué shapes toward the marked angled edges. Add any other quilting detail to your own satisfaction.

Trim the table runner to measure 10" x 38" and bind with the contrasting fabric to complete.

Trim the bell pull to measure 10" x 34", cutting the top edge straight across. Add a sleeve (page 79) and bind with the contrasting fabric to complete.

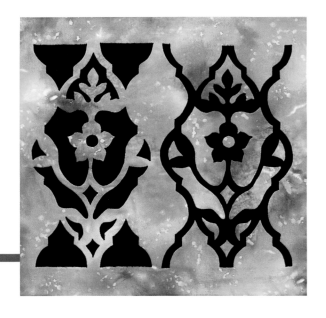

DIAMOND WINDOWS PILLOW, 16" x 16",
made with just the center portion of the
pattern by Val Jones, Hawarden, Flintshire, UK

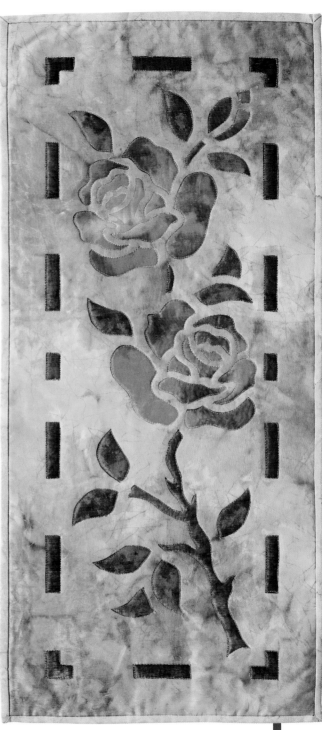

Positive   FRAMED ROSES WALLHANGINGS, 11" x 25", made by the author   Negative

FRAMED ROSES WALLHANGINGS

A delicate layer of colored chiffon overlays each of the wallhangings. It eliminates the need to appliqué around the edges of the cut shapes as they are secured during the quilting process.

This pretty project demonstrates how to highlight individual design elements inside the frame, such as flowers, stems, and leaves. To achieve this, the backing paper on the frame is only removed from behind the areas where the specific foundation fabric is to be fused. The process demands careful removal of the backing paper and precision cutting of the fabric shape before it is fused into place. The chiffon covering eliminates need for appliqué.

Review Chapter 3 for detailed Dual Image Appliqué instructions.

PINK AND BLUE DELIGHT, 11" x 24",
made by Eunice Lord, Amlwch, Anglesey, UK

REQUIREMENTS

Frame, fillers, and binding: ½ yard of light fabric
Foundations and binding: ½ yard of dark fabric
Roses and bud: rose fabric at least 7" x 14"
Leaves: green fabric at least 8" x 6"
Stems: brown fabric at least 10" x 6"
Border inserts: ⅛ yard
Sheer fabric (e.g., chiffon): 2 rectangles 12" x 26". Choose one sheer to enhance your light fabric and another to soften your dark fabric.
Batting for appliqué and quilting: 2 rectangles 15" x 29"
Backing and sleeves: 1 yard
Machine threads: to match the sheer fabrics

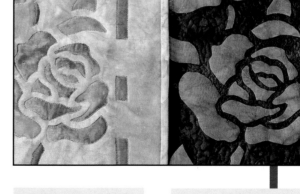

Negative   Positive

CUTTING

Light fabric:
1 rectangle 12" x 26"
2 strips 2" wide for the binding

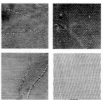

| Frame | Filler | Foundation Positive | Foundation Negative |

Dark fabric:
  1 rectangle 12" x 26"
  2 strips 2" wide for the binding
Border inserts:
  10 rectangles 1" x 2½"
  2 rectangles 1" x 1½"
  4 squares 1½" x 1½"
Backing:
  2 rectangles 15" x 29"
  2 rectangles 5" x 11" for the sleeves

Cut the fillers out accurately.

PREPARING THE FUSIBLE

Enlarge and trace the pattern (page 86) and sequence numbers onto the fusible web and trim away the excess fusible, leaving a ½" beyond the outer marked line. Fuse to the WS of the light filler/frame fabric. Allow it to cool.

Cut out the fillers. Keep them in sequence.

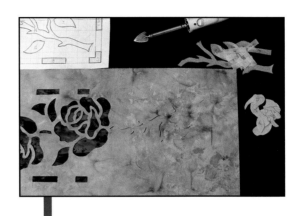

PREPARING THE PANELS

Center the frame, with the backing paper still on, RS up, onto the RS of the foundation.

Use the frame to position the fillers for fusing.

Remove the backing paper from the fillers and place them back in position within the frame. Use the tip of the iron to gently fuse the fillers in place. Remove the frame and fuse the fillers onto the foundation thoroughly to complete the positive panel.

Layer the panel with the batting and backing and position the dark chiffon layer over the top. Pin baste the layers together, ready for quilting.

Place the positive/filler panel on batting and backing and cover with a chiffon layer.

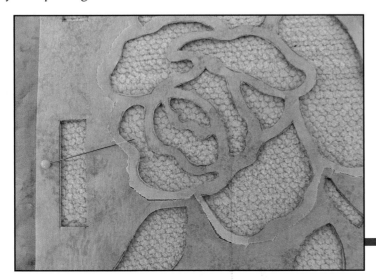

Score and lift the paper with a pin.

Secure the paper shape with pins; draw around the outside edge of the shape.

Fuse the flower shape in place on the exposed fusible.

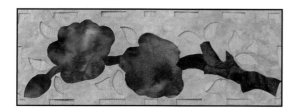

Fuse additional shapes in the same way.

TIP: Basting around the outside edge through all the layers helps to hold the chiffon in place.

On the negative/frame panel, additional fabric is added to highlight the roses, bud, leaves, and stems.

Place the frame on a cutting board with the paper side uppermost. Use a pin to score the paper all the way around the edge of one of the roses. If there is an adjacent shape, carefully score the paper halfway between the cut edges. Lift the paper by sliding the pin under it and gently remove it in one piece to reveal the exposed strip of fusible web underneath.

Without turning it over, place the paper shape onto the WS of a rose fabric. Pin it in place and draw around it accurately with a suitable marker.

TIP: Place the pins so that they don't go through the paper to distort it. Pin into the fabric on either side of the paper to form a bridge over it.

Cut the shape out, right on the marked line. Place it, WS uppermost, over the exposed fusible on the frame. Fuse in place.

Repeat the process for the second rose, the rose bud, stem, and leaves.

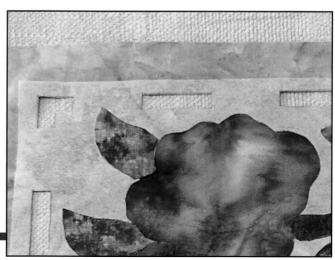

Remove the rest of the backing paper from the frame to expose the remaining fused fabric and position it on the foundation fabric. Place the precut border inserts behind the remaining holes. Cover them with a Teflon sheet (or baking parchment) and fuse all the shapes thoroughly to complete the negative panel.

Layer the panel with the batting and backing and position the light chiffon layer over the top. Pin baste the layers together, ready for quilting.

SEWING THE PANELS

On the positive/filler panel, free-motion quilt with a fine stipple stitch right up to the edges of the fused filler pieces.

On the negative/frame panel, straight stitch around the inside cut edges of the frame.

Trim the panels to measure 11" x 25". Add the sleeves (page 79) and bind (pages 80–82) to complete.

Place the negative/frame panel on batting and backing and cover with a chiffon layer.

The chiffon layer and quilting stitches secure the panel pieces.

FLORAL PATCHES QUILT, 52" x 52", made by the author

FLORAL PATCHES QUILT

FLORAL PATCHES, 50" x 50",
made by Jane Hatfield, Cheadle Hulme,
Cheshire, UK

Note: Trimmings from the foundation layer are used for the border inserts.

Don't be put off by the size and the apparent complexity of this project; it's easier than it looks! The dark frames and fillers are prepared in the usual way and each block of the quilt is worked independently for easy sewing.

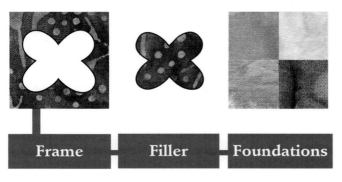

| Frame | Filler | Foundations |

It's the Four-Patch foundation layer of light and medium fabrics that provides an interesting twist to this project. Once the cut edges have been appliquéd, the quilt is constructed by sewing the blocks, with the light foundation squares adjacent to lights and the medium foundation squares adjacent to mediums, to produce an overall patchwork effect.

This project is great for using up smaller scraps of fabric, but you can use just two foundation fabrics to produce a more structured effect.

Review Chapter 3 for detailed Dual Image Appliqué instructions.

REQUIREMENTS

Frames, fillers, borders, and binding: 2½ yards of dark fabric
Foundations: 1⅛ yards total of a variety of light fabrics and 1⅛ yards total of a variety of medium fabrics
Fusible web: 1½ yards
Batting for appliqué: ¾ yard
Batting for quilting: 61" x 61"
Backing: 3⅝ yards
Machine threads: to match the dark fabric and a contrasting thread for the center circles

CUTTING

Dark fabric:
    17 strips 2" wide for the borders and binding
    13 squares 9½" x 9½" for the frames and fillers
    32 rectangles 1" x 4" for the middle pieced border
Light fabrics:
    50 squares 5" x 5"
Medium fabrics:
    50 squares 5" x 5"
Batting: 25 squares 8" x 8"
Fusible web: 13 squares 7½" x 7½"

Construct 25 Four-Patch blocks
for the foundations.

Iron the fusible centrally and
cut out the fillers accurately.

Pin the tips of the petals on the
seams and replace the fillers.

PREPARING THE FOUNDATIONS

Sort the foundation squares into sets of 2 lights and 2 mediums, with no repeats in each set.

Make 25 Four-Patch blocks. Press the seams from light to dark wherever possible.

PREPARING THE FUSIBLE

Trace the pattern centrally onto the 13 squares of fusible web so the web extends ½" beyond the outermost line. Fuse to the WS of the 13 dark squares. Allow them to cool.

Cut out the fillers, keeping each frame together with its fillers.

CONSTRUCTING THE BLOCKS

Center the frame, with backing paper still on, RS up, onto the RS of a Four-Patch foundation square. Use vertical pins to hold the tips of the petals to the seam lines.

Remove the backing paper from the fillers and place them back in position within the frame.

Use the tip of the iron to gently fuse the fillers in place. Remove the frame and fuse the fillers onto the foundation thoroughly to complete the positive block.

TIP: If you have chosen a patterned fabric, it is easier to place the fillers back into the frame because the pattern on the filler will exactly match the frame.

Remove the paper backing from the frame and fuse it onto the RS of a Four-Patch block. Fold back the border of the frame, right up to the fused edge, and use a ruler to cut away the extra foundation fabric to complete the negative block.

Keep the trimmed strips for the middle border.

Repeat these steps to make 25 blocks.

Pin baste each prepared block onto an 8" x 8" batting square and appliqué with a wide satin stitch.

Trim away the excess batting from beyond the outer line of stitches .

CONSTRUCTING THE QUILT

Use a design wall to arrange the squares in 5 rows of 5 blocks each, making sure that the light foundation squares are adjacent to light squares and medium squares are adjacent to mediums, with no repeated fabrics together.

Sew the blocks into rows and join the rows together.

Cut away the excess foundation fabric.

Make 13 frame blocks; make 12 filler blocks.

Appliqué with a wide satin stitch.

Trim away the excess batting.

The inner, pieced middle,
and outer border strips

ADDING THE BORDERS

Join the 2" wide strips end-to-end as needed and add an inner border to the quilt top (page 78).

For the pieced middle border, undo the seams of the strips trimmed from the Four-Patch foundations. Trim 28 pieces to measure 1" x 4".

Alternate 7 of these rectangles with 8 dark 1" x 4" rectangles and join them end-to-end, starting and finishing with a dark one. Line up the center light strip with the center square of the quilt and pin it with RS together onto the dark inner border. Pin the rest of the 1" strip to the inner border at intervals, leaving the extra dark fabric free at both corners.

Sew in place and trim away the excess fabric. In the same way, make and add the middle border to the remaining 3 sides.

Add an outer border with the remaining 2" wide strips.

FINISHING

Layer the completed top with the batting and backing and pin baste the layers together. Use a walking foot and straight stitch along the vertical and horizontal seams. Add close stippling around the centers of the flowers to hold them down.

The sample was quilted with a continuous cable pattern (page 88) that was marked before layering with the batting. Bind (pages 80–82) to complete.

INSIDE OUT, 57" x 76", made by
Iris Taylor, Penally, Tenby,
Pembrokeshire, UK

FLOWER & STEM CHRISTMAS QUILT, 48" x 48", made by the author

FLOWER & STEM CHRISTMAS QUILT

Review Chapter 3 for detailed Dual Image Appliqué instructions.

REQUIREMENTS

Frame, fillers, foundations, and binding: 2 yards of red fabric

Frame, fillers, and foundations: 2 yards of gold fabric

Fusible web: 1½ yards

Batting for appliqué: ¾ yard

Batting for quilting: 56" x 56"

Backing: 3⅜ yards

Machine threads: to match both fabrics

CUTTING

Red fabric:
  8 squares 8½" x 8½" for the center frames and fillers
  24 rectangles 4½" x 8½" for border blocks
  8 squares 4½" x 4½" for the corners
  6 strips 2" wide for the binding

Gold fabric:
  8 squares 8½" x 8½" for the center foundations
  8 squares 7½" x 7½" for the center foundations
  24 rectangles 4½" x 8½" for border blocks
  8 squares 4½" x 4½" for the corners

Batting:
  32 squares 7" x 7" batting

The warmth and the welcome of Christmas are reflected in the red and gold colors of this seasonal quilt. You can use the delicate flower motif and the basic dual image appliqué to make blocks for a pretty pillow, a colorful wallhanging, or the center of the quilt in this project.

The blocks surrounding the center illustrate the striking contrasts that can be produced with a little extra preparation. It's as simple as constructing the frame/filler and foundation squares from rectangles of red and gold before following the dual image appliqué.

| Frame | Filler | Foundation |

Iron the fusible onto the
WS of the fabric squares.

TIP: If you have to draw a quantity of motifs, it is worth preparing an accurate template.

PREPARING THE FUSIBLE

Enlarge and trace the flower pattern (page 87) and the centering lines onto the fusible 16 times, leaving about 1" between each motif. Cut them out, leaving a ½" beyond the marked edges.

PREPARING THE CENTER SQUARES

Center the marked fusible on the WS of the 8½" red squares and fuse in place. Allow them to cool.

Cut out the fillers and center circles.

TIP: There are 2 fillers within the frames for this project. The flowers are used to make the positive blocks and the centers are used with the frames to make the negative blocks.

Put the frame onto the foundation and replace the filler.

Center the frame, with backing paper still on, RS up, onto the RS of a gold 8½" square. Remove the backing paper from the filler and place it back in position within the frame.

Use the tip of the iron to gently fuse it in place. Remove the frame and fuse the filler to the foundation more thoroughly.

Remove the backing paper from the frame and fuse it, RS up, onto the RS of a 7½" gold square.

To position the center circle, reverse the paper backing from the filler and place it back inside the frame. Peel the paper off the circle and fuse it in place.

Use the backing paper to position the center circle.

Trim away the excess
fabric from the back.

Use a light box to carefully remove the excess gold fabric from beyond the fused edge.

Repeat the above method to make 8 frame blocks and 8 filler blocks.

Make 8 frame blocks.
Make 8 filler blocks.

MAKING THE BORDER BLOCKS

Make 24 squares measuring 8½" x 8½" by joining the red and gold 4½" x 8½" rectangles. Iron the seams toward the red. Mark the vertical center line on the WS and place it onto an ironing surface with marked side uppermost.

Match the center lines on the fusible pattern with the marked vertical line and the horizontal center seam of the foundation, and secure the fusible with vertical pins. Always place the flower on the gold section and the stem and leaf on the red section.

Fuse the flower in place and allow it to cool. Cut out the fillers, keeping them together with their frames.

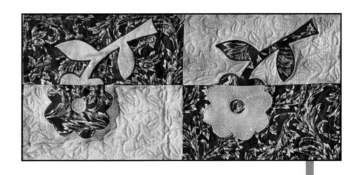

Make 8 frame border blocks.
Make 8 filler border blocks.

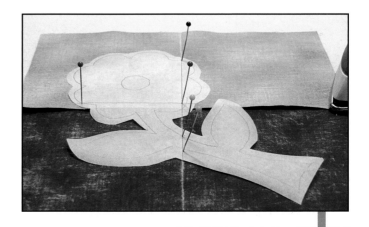

Secure and fuse the pattern
onto the WS of the fabric.

Place the frame, with backing paper still on, RS up onto the RS of another red and gold square, reversing the colors. Butt the seam allowances across the center. Remove the paper from the filler to position it accurately within the frame and secure it with vertical pins.

Remove the frame to double check the placement along the center seam before fusing the filler in place thoroughly. Accurate placement is essential!

Remove the paper from the frame and position and fuse it to another red and gold square with the colors reversed. Use the reversed backing paper from the filler to position the center circle.

Carefully cut away the excess fabric from beyond the fused edge on the back with the help of a light box.

Pin a batting square behind each motif and machine appliqué with a close zigzag stitch and matching thread.

TIP: Using the same thread for both fabrics is the easiest option. If you prefer to match thread with fabric, pay particular attention to where one fabric ends and the other begins.

On the WS, trim away the excess batting from beyond the outer line of stitches.

Use the 4½" squares to construct 4 Four-Patch corner blocks.

Place the frame onto a foundation, with colors reversed, and replace the filler.

Remove the frame and fuse thoroughly.

Sew around the cut edges.

Trim away the excess batting.

Make 4 corner blocks.

CONSTRUCTING THE QUILT

Use a design wall to arrange the blocks. Refer to the quilt photo (page 51). Sew the blocks into rows, then join the rows. Make sure that the seams butt up to one another for clean lines and accurate color changes.

Piece the backing as necessary. Place the quilt top onto batting and backing and pin baste. Quilt from the center to the edges. The sample is quilted with threads that match the fabrics for a textured effect. Bind (pages 80–82) to complete.

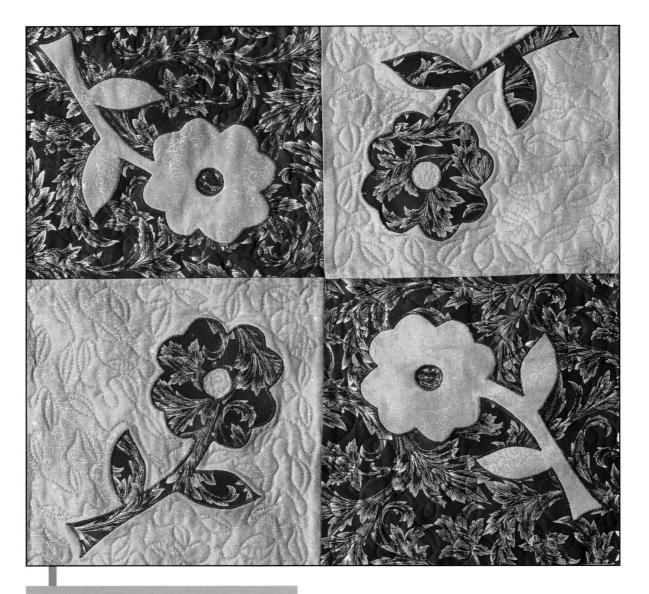

Quilt the blocks.

STRIPPY WALLHANGING, 4" x 31", 4" x 32", 5" x 33", 4" x 32", 4" x 31", made by the author

STRIPPY WALLHANGING

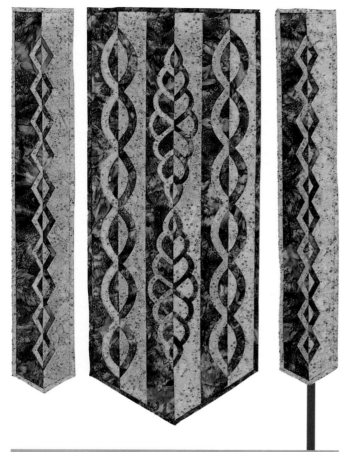

TWIST AND TURN, 24" x 35",
made by Liz Pedley, Burton-upon-Stather,
Lincolnshire, UK

As quilters, we occasionally find innovative patterns right under our noses, just by looking at something in a different way. The cable quilting pattern is a perfect example. The cables can be drafted as stencils with cut-out shapes and used to add an exciting and attractive twist to dual image appliqué projects.

Each pattern panel was sewn as a separate hanging, but they can also be constructed as a combined center panel with two outer strips, or all sewn together to make one larger wallhanging like the one shown to the left. Whatever your choice, the end results are striking!

Review Chapter 3 for detailed Dual Image Appliqué instructions.

REQUIREMENTS

Frames, fillers, foundations, backings, and bindings: 1 yard of red fabric and 1 yard of green fabric
Fusible: 1 yard
Batting: 4 strips 8" x 40" and 1 strip 9" x 40"
Backing fabric: 1 yard
Machine threads: to match both fabrics
Tassels: 3 skeins each of red and green embroidery floss

CUTTING

From both green and red fabrics:
6 strips 2½" x 36" for the outer/diamond and rope panels
2 strips 3" x 37" and 1 strip 3" x 15" for the center/plaited cable panel
Cut 5 strips at 1¼" x 40" for single binding strips
From the backing fabric:
4 strips 8" x 40"
1 strip 9" x 40"

| Frame | Filler | Foundations |

PREPARING THE FUSIBLE

TIP: There are 2 different fillers within the frames. The intact cable is the outer filler, used to make the positive panel. The centers are the inner fillers, used with the frame to make the negative panel.

Enlarge and trace the 3 cable patterns (page 88) and the center lines onto the fusible web. Cut them out ½" beyond the outer marked line. Number the fillers in sequence for ease of placement later.

PREPARING THE ROPE AND DIAMOND PANELS

Make strip-sets with the red and green strips, RS together, matching the sizes. Press the seam allowances toward the red, making sure there are no tucks in the seams (so important for accuracy!).

On the WS, put a pin in the seam, 2" down from the top edge of the strip. Match the tip of the fusible rope pattern with the pin and line up the center line of the pattern with the seam. Use vertical pins to secure the pattern on the fabric. Use the tip of the iron to fuse the pattern to the fabric along the center seam before ironing the rest thoroughly. Allow it to cool.

Cut out the fillers. Make sure that the inward and outward points are right on the seam.

Fuse the pattern along
the center seam.

Cut the fillers out accurately.

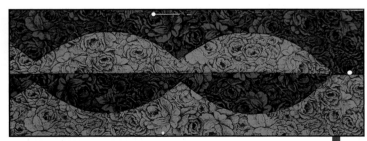

Put the frame on the foundation
with colors reversed.

Place the cable filler into the frame
and pin the center seams.

With its paper still on, place the frame, RS up, onto the RS of a foundation strip, with the colors reversed. Check that the edges of the frame and foundation are aligned and that the center seams are butted up where appropriate. Use vertical pins to secure the layers together.

Carefully remove the paper from the intact cable filler so the paper can be reused. Put the cable filler into the frame, making sure that the seams are butted along their length. Use vertical pins to hold the layers together.

Remove the frame and fuse the filler to complete the positive panel.

Remove the paper from the frame and place it, RS up, on top of the RS of another foundation strip, with colors reversed. Press to fuse.

Place the paper backing from the intact cable filler, WS up, inside the frame. Remove the papers from the individual inner fillers and pin them back in sequence. Remove the paper pattern, check that all the seams are aligned, and fuse.

Use a light box to carefully remove the excess fabric from beyond the fused edge on the back to complete the negative panel.

Repeat this procedure to make positive and negative diamond panels.

Remove the frame and fuse the filler.

Fuse the frame onto the fabric and use the backing paper to place the individual fillers.

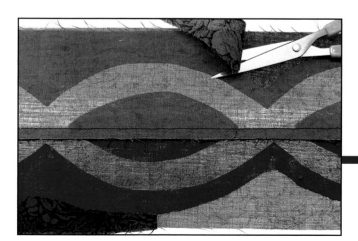

Trim away the excess
fabric from the back.

PREPARING THE PLAITED CABLE PANEL

Following the same procedure for aligning the seams, fuse the plaited cable pattern 2" from the top edge of the red and green strip-set. Cut out the intact cable filler and individual center fillers.

Put a pin in the seam 3½" down from the lower edge of the cut-out frame and fuse the intact cable filler along the center seam. Fuse the remaining 15" strip of red and green fabric as a foundation behind the frame, reversing the colors.

Use the paper backing from the intact cable to place the center fillers. Fuse thoroughly. Remove the excess fabric from the back.

Place each strip onto the prepared batting and backing strips to appliqué and quilt at the same time with a small zigzag stitch, using a black thread to complement both fabrics. Echo quilt using matching threads.

SHAPING THE TAPERED ENDS

Trim the center panel to measure 5" wide and the outer 4 panels to measure 4" wide. Trim the top edges to measure 1" from the start of the patterns.

To shape the lower edges, make a mark on the seam 2" from the end of the pattern. Place the 1" line of a ruler to run along the side of the pattern, angled toward the mark, and use a cutter along the edge of the ruler to trim away the excess fabric. Repeat the process to shape the other side.

FINISHING

Add hanging sleeves, rings, or loops to the back as preferred and bind (pages 80–82) so that red is sewn to green and green is sewn to red. A tassel can be added to emphasize the length.

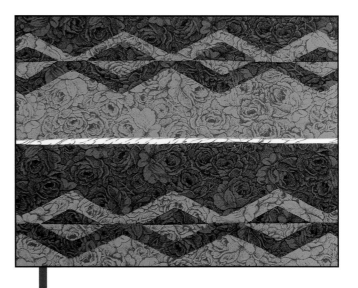
The fused diamond panels

Fuse the pattern.

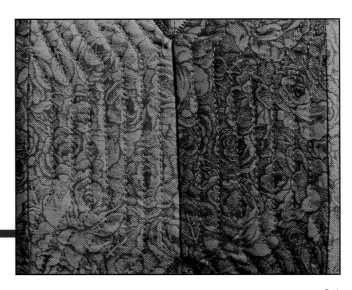

Echo quilting

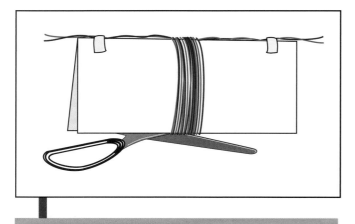

Making the tassels

MAKING A TASSEL

Use both colors to make a 3" tassel.

Cut out a 6" square of cardstock and fold it in half (6" x 3").

Cut a 12" length of embroidery floss from both colors and place them centrally along the folded edge of the cardboard using masking tape to secure at the ends.

Wrap both colors of floss around the card until half of the skein has been used.

Remove the masking tape to release the threads and tie them tightly and securely to hold the threads together.

Ease the scissors into the open edge of the card to cut through the floss.

Create the head by wrapping 2 more 12" lengths of floss tightly around the cut threads, ¾" down from the top of the tassel. Knot tightly and either trim the ends or weave them into the tassel with a needle.

ORANGES AND LEMONS, 10" x 36", made by Val Jones, Hawarden, Flintshire, UK

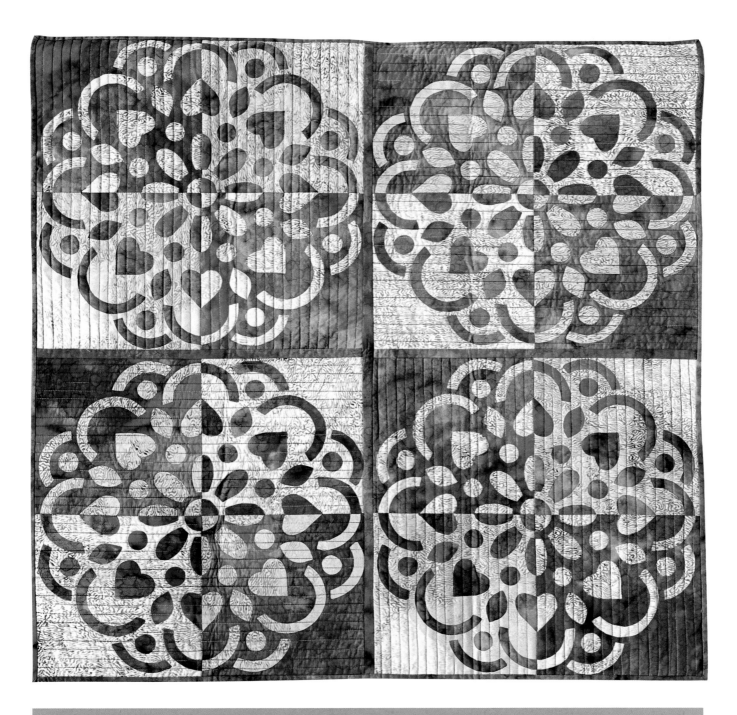

DOILY LAP QUILT, 36" x 36", made by the author

DOILY LAP QUILT

The complexity and size of the pattern pieces in this project make it more of a challenge to prepare and sew, but the delightful results make the extra effort well worth it. Four-Patch blocks are used for both the frame/filler and foundation fabrics. The blocks are quilted individually, then sewn together.

Review Chapter 3 for detailed Dual Image Appliqué instructions.

REQUIREMENTS

Frames, fillers, foundations, joining strips, and bindings: 1¼ yards of dark fabric and 1 yard of light fabric
Batting: four squares 20" x 20"
Backing: 1¼ yards

STRIPPY DOILIES, 36" x 36",
made by Dot Aellan, Heald Green, Cheshire, UK

Trace the pattern onto the fusible

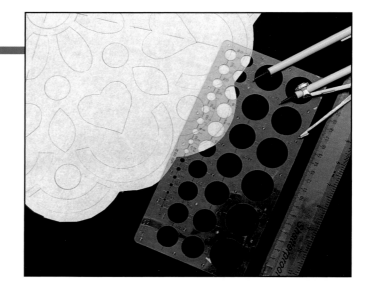

CUTTING

From both the light and dark fabrics:
6 squares 10" x 10" each (12 total)
Dark fabric:
2 strips 1" wide for the front joining strips
4 strips 2" wide for the double-fold binding
Backing fabric:
4 squares 20" x 20"
2 strips 1¼" wide for the back joining strips
Machine thread: variegated thread

PREPARING THE FUSIBLE

Enlarge and trace the pattern (page 89) onto the paper side of the fusible web. Trim away the extra fusible leaving ½" beyond the outer marked line.

Frame

Filler

Foundations

Press the seams from light to dark.

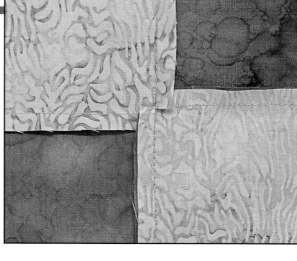

Use a compass and stencil to draw accurate circles. Mark the center lines and number the fillers to help with placement later.

PREPARING THE BLOCKS

Make 6 Four-Patch blocks with the 10" squares of light and dark fabrics. Clip the center seam so the seam allowances can be pressed toward the dark fabric. Make sure there are no tucks in the seams.

Four of the Four-Patch blocks act as foundations; the remaining 2 blocks produce the frames and fillers for the blocks.

Center the marked fusible on the WS of the Four-Patch blocks, matching the center lines on the fusible with the seams. Use vertical pins to secure the pattern. Fuse in place. Allow them to cool.

Cut out the fillers, making sure that the inward and outward points are right on the seam where appropriate.

With its paper still on, center the frame on a Four-Patch foundation block, making sure that the colors are reversed and the outer edges are aligned. Butt the seams and pin along their length to secure them.

Remove the paper backings from the fillers and place them back into position within the frame, butting and pinning the seams. Fuse the fillers in place to complete the positive block.

Remove the backing paper from the frame and position it onto another Four-Patch foundation block, with colors reversed. Pin it accurately and press to fuse the layers together.

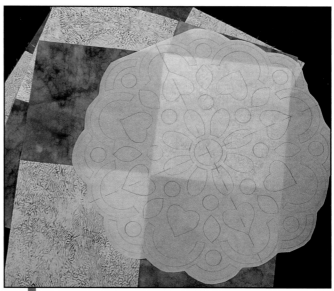

Use 3 Four-Patch blocks to produce 2 patterned blocks.

Pin the center lines of the fusible along the seams.

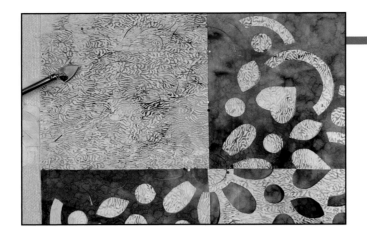

Fuse the fillers onto a
foundation with colors reversed.

From the back, carefully trim away the excess fabric beyond the fused edge with the help of a light box to complete the negative block.

Repeat the steps again for a total of 4 blocks and arrange them in sequence on a design wall.

Mark quilting lines that run parallel to the center seam at 1" intervals, either parallel with or at right angles to the quilting lines on the adjacent blocks.

TIP: If the project is going to be well-used and laundered, secure the cut edges with a zigzag stitch in addition to or instead of the straight-line quilting.

Use a walking foot to quilt the blocks.

Place each block onto the batting and backing squares and pin baste the layers together. Use a walking foot to quilt along the marked lines with a variegated thread, working from the center seam towards the edges, alternating the direction of sewing. Then quilt between the lines so the quilting lines are spaced ½" apart.

TIP: A walking foot or even-feed foot is recommended for this repetitive type of sewing because it feeds the layers evenly under the needle.

Trim the blocks to measure 18" x 18".

JOINING THE PRE-QUILTED SQUARES

Trim a 1" front and 1¼" back joining strip to the size of the quilted block.

Place the 1" front joining strip, RS together, onto the lower edge of the RS of block A. At the same time, place the 1¼" back joining strip, RS together, on the back of the same edge.

Joining sequence
Front joining strip   back joining strip

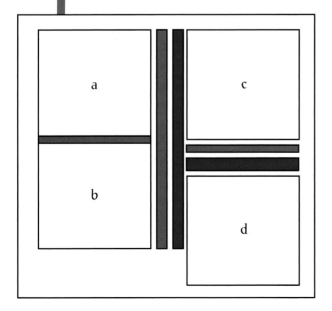

Sew the front and back joining
strips at the same time.

Pin well at right angles to the edge and sew them in place with a very accurate ¼" seam allowance. On the RS, press only the top strip to cover the seam.

TIP: These joining ¼" seams must be accurate. A larger seam allowance makes the edges of the blocks overlap and a smaller seam allowance leaves a gap between the blocks.

Place block A, with RS together, onto block B, making sure that the patterns are aligned. Match the raw edge of the front joining strip on block A with the edge of block B and sew in place with a very accurate ¼" seam.

Turn to the WS and lay it flat. You'll see that the raw edges of the blocks neatly abut each other.

Press the back joining strip to cover the join, and fold under a small seam allowance along the back joining strip to cover the line of stitches. Sew this down by hand to complete.

Repeat with blocks C and D.

Trim the remaining 1" front and 1¼" back joining strips to the size of the two-block units and join as before. Bind (pages 80–82) to complete.

Sew the front joining strip
of block A to block B.

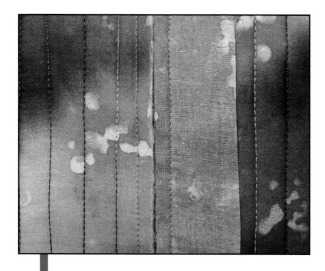

The raw edges are brought
together on the WS.

Hand sew along the folded
fabric on the back.

BOSTON FALL WALLHANGING, 33" x 40", made by the author

BOSTON FALL WALLHANGING

Frame   Filler   Foundations

TURQUOISE DELIGHT PILLOW, 16" x 16"
made by Kath Lloyd, Drury, Flintshire, UK

I made this quilt after returning from a trip to see the magnificent autumnal colors in New England. Nothing can prepare you for the scale of mother nature's exhibition, the variety of her palette, and the intensity of her colors; it was simply breathtaking! I collected and pressed a maple leaf and used it to make the leaf pattern for this project.

Combining the leaf shape with a diagonal seam produces a dynamic, seasonal wall quilt.

Review Chapter 3 for detailed Dual Image Appliqué instructions.

REQUIREMENTS

Frames, fillers, and foundations:
   1 yard total of a variety of light reds and oranges
   1 yard total of dark greens and browns
Inner border and binding: ½ yard of black fabric
Outer border: ¼ yard of autumn fabric
Fusible: 1 yard
Batting for appliqué: 20 squares 6" x 6"
Batting for quilting: 37" x 44"
Backing: 37" x 44"
Machine thread: black

CUTTING

Lights and darks:
   15 squares 8½" x 8½" light reds and oranges, cut in half on the diagonal
   15 squares 8½" x 8½" dark greens and browns, cut in half on the diagonal
Black fabric:
   2 strips 1" x 34" and 2 strips 1" x 40" for the inner borders
   4 strips 2" wide for the binding
Border fabric: 4 strips 2½" wide

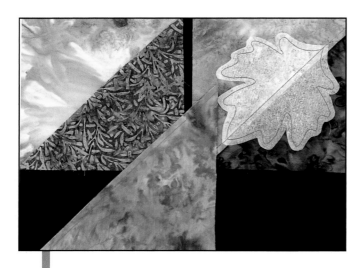

Prepare the fusible and select the triangles.

Sew a light triangle to a
dark triangle and fuse
the pattern in place.

Cut the filler out
of the frame.

PREPARING THE FUSIBLE

Enlarge and trace the leaf pattern (page 87) and centering line onto the fusible 20 times, leaving 1" between each one. Cut them out, leaving a ½" seam allowance beyond the marked edges.

Pair a light triangle with a dark triangle and sew each pair together.

TIP: You will be sewing along a bias edge so let the machine feed the fabrics through without resistance. Pulling can distort and stretch a bias edge.

Press the seam allowances toward the dark. Center the fusible pattern along the diagonal seam on the WS and fuse it in place. Allow it to cool.

Cut out the fillers.

PREPARING THE BLOCKS

With its paper still on, center a frame onto a foundation square with the light and dark reversed. Butt the seams together along the diagonal.

Remove the backing paper from the filler and place it back in position inside the frame, butting the diagonal seams with those of the foundation square. Secure with vertical pins. Remove the frame, check the diagonals, and fuse the filler to complete the positive block.

Use the frame to position the filler.

Remove the backing paper from the frame and center it, RS up on a foundation square, butting up the diagonals. Press to fuse.

Use a light box to remove the excess foundation fabric from the back to complete the negative block.

Repeat to produce 10 positive and 10 negative blocks.

Pin baste each block onto the small batting squares and satin stitch around the cut edges with black thread. From the back, trim away the excess batting from around the edges of the stitches.

Line up the diagonal line on a square ruler with the diagonal seam and trim the blocks to measure 7½" x 7½".

CONSTRUCTING THE QUILT

Arrange the blocks in 5 rows of 4 blocks each. Sew the blocks into rows and join the rows to complete the center of the quilt.

Use the 1" black strips to add an inner border to the quilt top (page 78). Use the 2" autumn fabric strips to add the outer border to the quilt.

Pin the quilt top onto batting and backing ready for quilting. A minimal amount of quilting is necessary to hold the layers together—a straight stitch in the ditch between the blocks and a herringbone stitch along the diagonal seams. Square up the quilt.

Prepare a hanging sleeve (page 79) and bind (pages 80–82) to complete.

Fuse the frame.

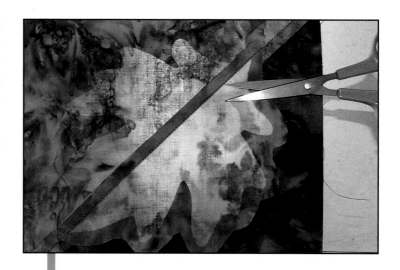

Trim away the excess fabric from the back.

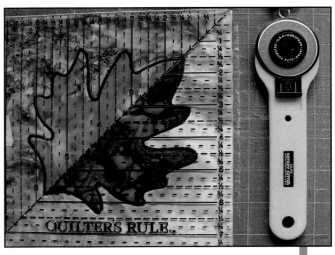

Trim away the excess batting
after stitching the edges.

Trim all the blocks to the same size.

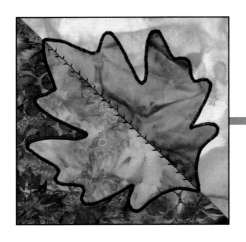

Herringbone
stitching used
along the
diagonals

Close-up of maple leaves

New England fall

FLOWER WHEEL QUILT, 78" x 93½", made by the author

FLOWER WHEEL QUILT

FLOWER WHEEL QUILT, 78" x 93½"

I happily confess that this quilt is constructed with a selection of light and dark fabrics from my favorite part of the color wheel. It is a great project for using up fat quarters of many different fabrics, as is detailed in the method below, but the pretty Flower Wheel motif looks equally good with just two fabrics.

The method is the same, but the fillers, frames, and foundations are made from quarter-square triangles.

TIP: If you want to alter the size of this quilt, be aware that it takes 3 quarter-square triangle units to make 2 blocks. You need to prepare 30 such units for this 20-block quilt.

Review Chapter 3 for detailed Dual Image Appliqué instructions.

REQUIREMENTS

Frames, fillers, foundations, and striped borders: 15 fat quarters of dark fabrics and 15 fat quarters of light fabrics
Batting for appliqué: 2 yards
Batting for quilting: 86" x 102"
Backing fabric: 8¾ yards
Inner and outer borders and binding: 3 yards
Fusible web: 20 squares at 14½" x 14½" or 8½ yards
Machine threads: variegated thread to complement all the fabrics or threads to match the individual fabrics

TIP: This quilt can be constructed as prequilted blocks and joined with narrow strips, as detailed in DOILY LAP QUILT project (page 63). If you prefer to do this, omit the 14½" x 14½" batting squares and prepare 20 batting and backing squares of 20" x 20" so that you can appliqué and quilt the blocks at the same time.

CUTTING

From both light and dark fabrics:
15 squares 17½" x 17½" cut along both diagonals to produce 4 triangles.
74 rectangles 2½" x 5½" for the striped border
Batting for appliqué:
20 squares 14½" x 14½"
Border fabric:
From the 3 yard length, parallel to the selvage, cut:
4 strips 1½" wide for the inner border
4 strips 2½" wide for the outer border
4 strips 2" wide for the binding
From the remaining fabric, cut 4 corner squares 5½" x 5½".
Backing:
3 lengths of fabric 102"

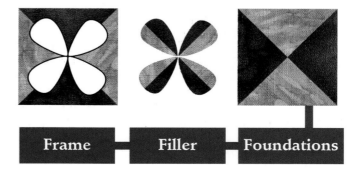

Frame | Filler | Foundations

Cutting large squares accurately

TIP: When cutting squares larger than an available ruler, make a card template to the required size. Iron 4 fabrics together, making sure that the edges are even and the grains match. Place them onto a large cutting mat. Put the template on top, with its edges parallel to those of the fabrics, and mark dots on the top fabric at the corners of the template. Remove the template and cut from dot to dot with a sharp rotary cutter and long ruler. If the fabrics haven't been disturbed, cut the squares along the diagonals to produce 4 triangles.

PREPARING THE FUSIBLE

Enlarge and trace the pattern (page 89) and centering lines onto the fusible web 20 times. Cut them out ½" beyond the outer marked line.

PREPARING THE BLOCKS

Pair up 2 matching light triangles with 2 matching dark triangles to construct the quarter-square triangle units. Press the seams toward the dark fabrics, clipping the center seam to allow this to happen.

TIP: You will be sewing along bias edges so let the machine feed the fabrics through without resistance. Pulling can distort and stretch a bias edge.

TIP: As you are pressing the seams, take time to sort the squares into sets of 3, with no repeated fabrics. This saves time during construction and may mean you won't have to make extra blocks later on.

Center the marked fusible on the WS of the quarter-square triangle blocks, matching the diagonal lines on the fusible with the seams. Use vertical pins to secure the pattern. Fuse in place. Allow them to cool.

Preparing the fusible and blocks

Press all seams from light to dark.

Align the diagonal pattern
lines with the seams.

Cut out the fillers, keeping them with their frames and their chosen foundations (the second and third quarter-square triangle in each set) until you are ready to fuse them.

With its paper backing still on, center the frame, RS up, on the RS of a foundation square. Make sure the light and dark fabrics are reversed. Use vertical pins to line up the centers and secure the butted seams.

Remove the backing papers from the fillers and put them back in the frame. Press gently to secure them.

Remove the frame and press the fillers thoroughly to fuse them in place. This completes the positive block.

Peel the paper from the back of the frame, pin, and fuse it to the other foundation square in the set. Use a light box to remove the excess foundation fabric from the back to complete the negative block.

Make 10 positive and 10 negative blocks.

Place each block onto a 14½" x 14½" batting square and appliqué the cut edges with a small stippling stitch.

From the back, trim away the excess batting beyond the outer stitches. Trim each block to measure.

Position the frame
onto the foundation.

CONSTRUCTING THE QUILT

Arrange the blocks in 4 rows of 5 blocks each. Sew the blocks into rows and join the rows.

Measure through the horizontal center, join the 1½" border strips to this length, and sew them in place. Measure through the vertical center and add the 1½" strips to the sides (page 78).

Place the fillers back into the frame.

Remove the frame and press thoroughly.

Measure again and join together enough 2½" x 5½" strips along the 5½" side to match these measurements for the pieced middle borders. Alternate the lights with the darks and iron all the seams in the same direction.

Add the top and bottom borders. Sew a 5½" x 5½" corner square to both ends of the side borders and add to the quilt.

Measure and add the outer border using the 2½" strips to complete the quilt top. Press carefully.

Place the completed top onto batting and backing and pin baste the layers together. A minimal amount of quilting is necessary to hold the layers together. Straight stitch along the diagonals, using a walking foot. Add close stippling around the centers of the flowers. Add decorative free-motion quilting along the vertical and horizontal seams with a large stippling stitch on the striped border.

Square up the quilt. Bind (pages 80–82) to complete.

Appliqué the cut edges.

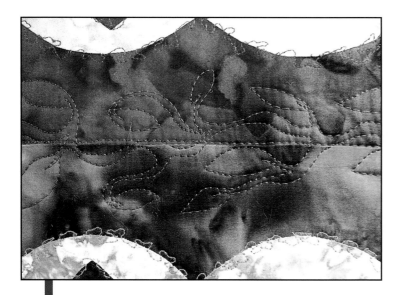

Decorative quilting along the seams

Trim away the excess batting.

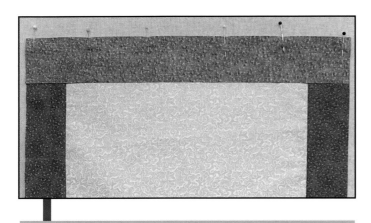

Adding straight borders

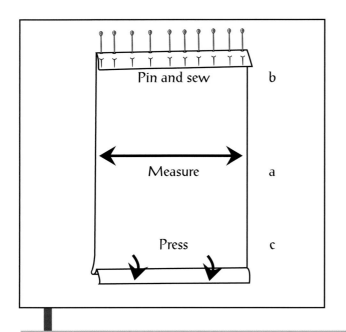

Adding the top and bottom
borders to a quilt

Note: Sewing threads and marked lines are contrasted and exaggerated for photography.

ADDING STRAIGHT BORDERS

Measure through the horizontal center of the completed top to get the length for the top and bottom borders (a). Cut 2 strips to this length by the chosen width.

TIP: The outer edges of a quilt are likely to have stretched during construction, so measuring through the centers of the quilt prevents wavy borders.

With RS together, place the border strip along the quilt edge, matching and pinning the center points. Pin the ends of the strips to the corners of the quilt and pin at regular intervals to make the quilt fit the border (b). Sew it in place with a ¼" seam allowance and press both seams away from the center (c).

Measure through the vertical center, which now includes the top and bottom borders. Cut the side strips to this length by the chosen width. Pin as before, sew, and press to complete the border.

USING SEE-THROUGH RULERS

The grid-marked transparent rulers that are available to quilters are invaluable. They are used with a rotary cutter and cutting board to cut accurate squares, rectangles, and strips in preparation for the projects. Being transparent, the vertical and horizontal lines on the ruler can be matched with those of the seams to produce straight edges and perfect corners as part of the finishing process. Regular quilting grids can be marked and points can be shaped specifically to the 30-, 45- and 60-degree angle lines.

SHAPING A TAPERED POINT

An easy way to shape a point is to put a dot, at a chosen distance (for example, 2") from the end of the appliqué, to give the required length to the wallhanging. Place the edge of the ruler on this dot and lay one of the horizontal lines (for example, 1") against the edge of the appliqué. Cut along the ruler with a cutter and repeat for the other side.

ATTACHING A HANGING SLEEVE

Cut a strip of backing fabric 5" wide by the width of the top (a). Fold under the short ends ¼" and ¼" again and stitch. Press under a ¼" seam along one long edge. Place the sleeve onto the back of the quilt, with RS up and the raw edges level. Put the pins in at right angles to the edge to secure the sleeve onto the back of the quilt (b); basting is optional.

Secure the sleeve during the binding process and sew down the turned lower edge by hand, using matching thread and concealed stitches (c).

If you prefer, you can prepare a double sleeve to protect the back of the quilt, cutting an 8½" wide strip.

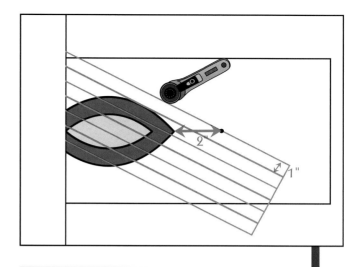

Shaping the points on a wallhanging

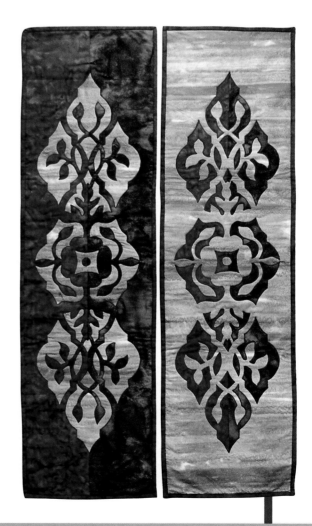

WELSH JEWELS, 9" x 33", made by June Barker, Low Moor, Yorkshire, UK

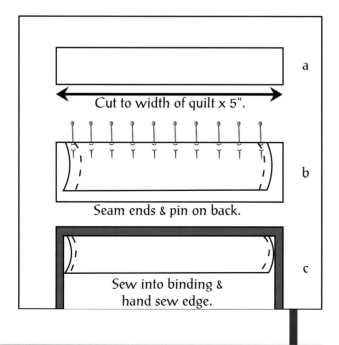

a

Cut to width of quilt x 5".

b

Seam ends & pin on back.

c

Sew into binding & hand sew edge.

Attaching a hanging sleeve

Joining binding strips

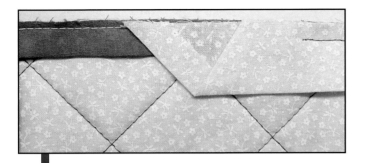

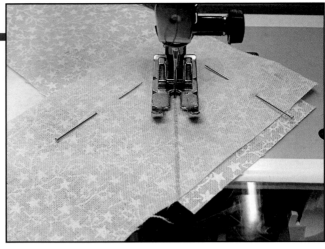

Starting to bind

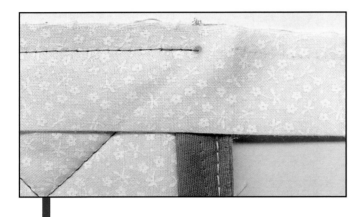

Stop sewing ¼" from the corner.

DOUBLE-FOLD STRAIGHT-CUT BINDING

Measure around the outside edge of the quilt and add 10". Cut 2" wide strips on the straight-of-grain to equal this measurement.

Sew the strips together with a diagonal (bias) seam, pinning 2 strips together, at right angles to one another.

Mark a 45-degree line from top left to bottom right and sew along it. Cut away the excess fabric on the corner to leave a ¼" seam. Press the seam open.

Fold the binding strip in half lengthwise, WS together.

Cut the starting edge of the binding strip at a 45-degree angle, and press under a ¼" seam allowance to tidy the edge.

Place the start of the strip about 5" from a corner, matching the raw edges of the strip with those of the quilt. Leave 3" free at the start of the binding to give space for the overlap and machine sew it in place with an accurate ¼" seam.

Create an angle on the corner.

Mark a dot on the binding exactly ¼" from the first corner and stop sewing at the dot. Reverse for a few stitches and remove the corner from under the pressure foot.

Pull the binding away from the corner at a 45-degree angle

Fold the binding back down toward you so that the raw edges of the binding lie along the next edge to be sewn. The fold of the tuck must be level with the raw edges at the corner.

TIP: If the tuck is too low, the corner will be flattened; if the tuck is too high, the corner will be elongated.

Resume sewing from the top of the tuck. After turning the final corner, trim the end of the binding to match the 45-degree angle at the start of the binding, overlapping the folded edge by about 1". Slide the trimmed end inside the folded end and finish sewing the seam.

Turn the binding onto the back of the quilt and sew the folded edge down with a matching thread and concealed stitches, mitering the extra fabric at the corners. Sew the overlapped seam by hand to complete.

To turn a corner of more than 90 degrees, take a small tuck in the binding strip to make the fold lie centrally and equidistant from both sides.

To bind a sharp corner, mark a dot on the fabric that is ¼" from both angled sides. Stop at the dot, reverse and remove the edge from under the pressure foot. Make an exaggerated tuck and start sewing the next side at the same dot, without sewing over the tuck.

Sew a tuck on the corner.

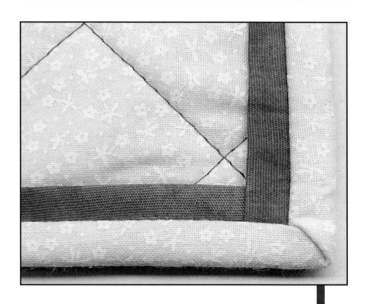

The mitered corner

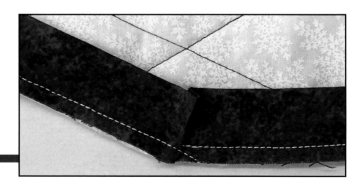

Binding a wide corner

If you need to bind with two different fabrics, attach and trim the first binding strip and sew the folded edge onto the back by hand. Attach the second binding strip, sewing across the first at the point. Trim away the extra fabric to leave ½" beyond the point.

Turn the raw edges under on the point with a large needle or stiletto and sew them down.

USING A LIGHT BOX

Although not essential, a light box is very useful. It is specifically used in the dual image appliqué to trim away the excess fabric from the back after fusing. A table lamp without a shade, placed under a glass-topped table, is a simple way to create a light box.

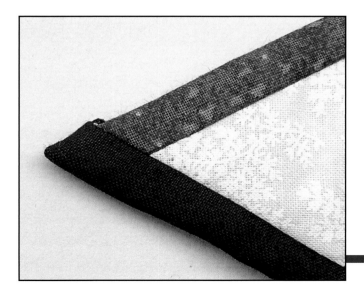

Binding with two fabrics

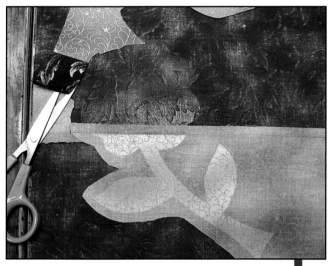

Working on a light box

Turn the seam allowance at the point.

PATTERNS

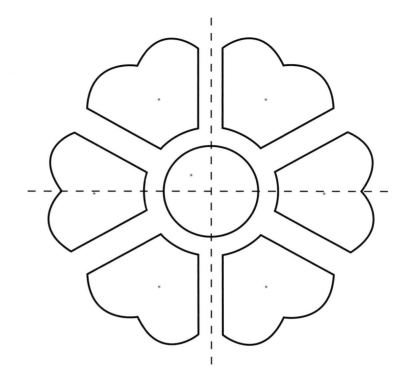

Chapter 1–Page 10
Shown at 50% of actual size
Enlarge this pattern 200%

Chapter 3–Page 17
Shown at 80% of actual size
Enlarge this pattern 125%

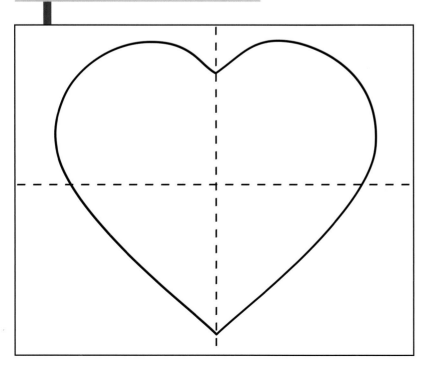

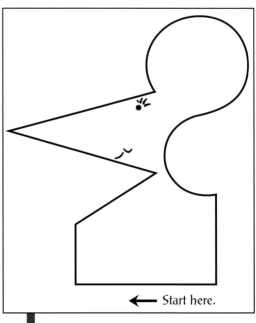

← Start here.

Chapter 3–Page 19
Shown at 80% of actual size
Enlarge this pattern 125%

Inner
filler

Center

* Inner filler is
used with the
frame to create
the negative
pattern.

Chapter 4 – Page 26
MOSAIC FLOWERS TOTE BAGS
Shown at 33% of actual size
Enlarge this pattern 300%

Chapter 4 – Page 26
MOSAIC FLOWERS TOTE BAGS
Shown at 33% of actual size
Enlarge this pattern 300%

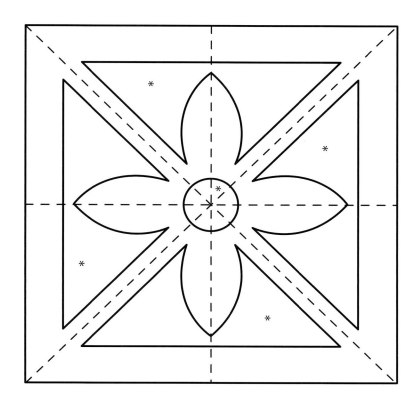

Chapter 4 – Page 46
FLORAL PATCHES QUILT
Shown at 50% of actual size
Enlarge this pattern 200%

Chapter 4 – Page 32
CAT IN THE WINDOW
Shown at 25% of actual size
Enlarge this pattern 400%

Chapter 4 – Page 36
BELL PULL WALLHANGING
Shown at 25% of actual size
Enlarge this pattern 400%

Chapter 4 – Page 41
FRAMED ROSES WALLHANGING
Shown at 25% of actual size
Enlarge this pattern 400%

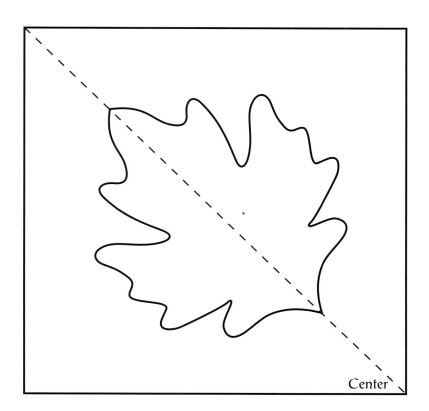

Center

Center

Chapter 4 – Page 68
BOSTON FALL WALLHANGING
Shown at 50% of actual size
Enlarge this pattern 200%

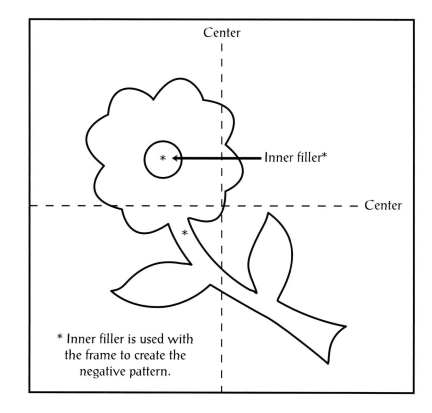

Center

Inner filler*

Center

Chapter 4 – Page 51
FLOWER & STEM CHRISTMAS QUILT
Shown at 50% of actual size
Enlarge this pattern 200%

* Inner filler is used with
the frame to create the
negative pattern.

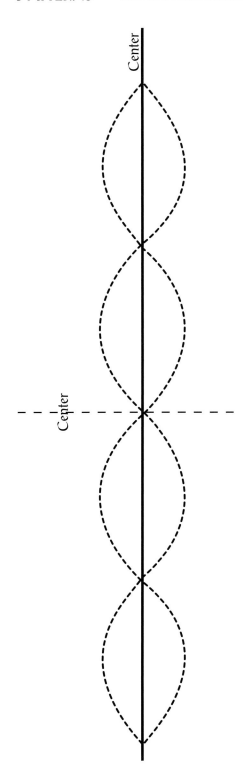

Chapter 4 – Page 46
FLORAL PATCHES quilting pattern
shown at 80% of actual size
Enlarge this pattern 125%

Chapter 4 – Page 57 STRIPPY WALLHANGING
Shown at 25% of actual size
Enlarge this pattern 400%

Center

Center

Center

Chapter 4 – Page 63
DOILY LAP QUILT
Shown at 25% of actual size
Enlarge this pattern 400%

Center

Center

Center

Chapter 4 – Page 73
FLOWER WHEEL QUILT
Shown at 33% of actual size
Enlarge this pattern 300%

GALLERY

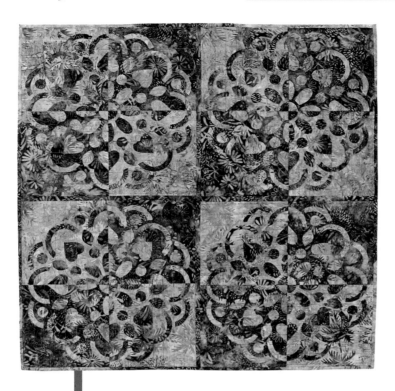

PAULINE'S PURPLE WROUGHT IRON,
16" x 16" each, made by Pauline Brown,
Knockin Heath, Oswestry, Shropshire, UK

DILYS' DOILIES, 36" x 36",
made by Florine Schultz Johnson,
Clarksville, GA

SPRING BUTTERFLIES WALLHANGING,
26¼" x 26¼", made by Pauline Brown,
Knockin Heath, Oswestry, Shropshire, UK

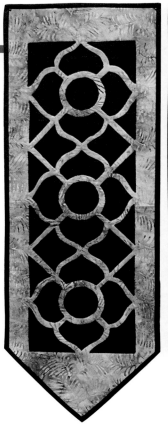

WINDOWS: SUNSET (positive),
SUNRISE (negative), 10" x 28½", each
made by Celia McTeer, Churchdown,
Gloucestershire, UK

YING AND YANG, 10" x 30",
made by Beth Stephenson,
Cleckheaton, West Yorkshire, UK

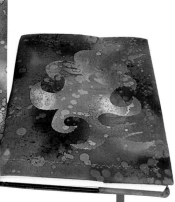

DOODLE BOOK COVERS, 5¾" x 8¼",
made by Jennifer Ellis,
Treuddyn, Flintshire, UK

DAISIES AT DAWN
13" x 21½", made by
Judith Ayton,
Green Norton,
Northamptonshire, UK

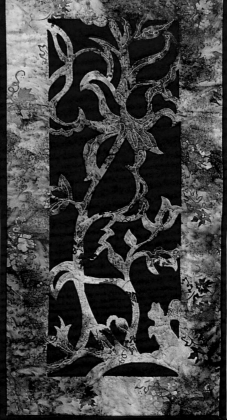

JACOBEAN POSITIVE AND
NEGATIVE, 11" x 23",
made by Helen Bailey
Longridge,
Lancashire, UK

RESOURCES

BIBLIOGRAPHY

All About Quilting from A to Z
C&T Publishing; Lafayette, CA 2002

The Complete Book of Patchwork, Quilting, and Appliqué, by
Linda Seward and Mitchell Beazley; London, UK 1987

Heirloom Machine Quilting by Harriet Hargrave
C&T Publishing; Lafayette, CA 1995

QUILTING ORGANIZATIONS

American Quilter's Society (AQS)
www.americanquilter.com

The National Quilt Museum (NQM)
www.quiltmuseum.org

International Quilt Association
www.quilts.org

Quilts Inc.
www.quilts.com

Quilters' Guild of the British Isles
www.quiltersguild.org.uk

Twisted Thread
www.twistedthread.com

Grosvenor Exhibitions Ltd
www.grosvenorexhibitions.co.uk

HIGH SUMMER BUTTERFLIES, 14" x 14", each
made by Brenda Farmhill,
Burnley, Lancashire, UK

SUNFLOWER, 14" x 14", each
made by Ruth Wallet,
Clipston, Northamptonshire, UK

A "painterly" picture made with fabric circles and rectangles, fused onto a foundation layer. Textural machine quilting through a cotton batting adds decorative detail.

AUTHOR'S POSTSCRIPT

A lot of precious time and effort goes into writing a book and there is great pleasure to be gained from conveying an idea concisely, through text and illustration, for the readers. Backed with the confidence that only years of experience can give, it takes many months of concentrated application to design appropriate projects, to source the right fabrics, and to fine-tune the teaching methods. But, when all that's said and done, I'd really rather be sewing!

And so now I happily retreat from the cold, un-emotional face and harsh keyboard of my computer screen and return to the warmth of my colorful and welcoming fabrics that have been waiting patiently in the wings. It's true to say that I feel a quilt coming on and PANSIES is a taster of the explosion of color that's just around my next corner!

MEET DILYS FRONKS

"Dilys the Quilt," as she is known in Wales, may have come to quilting as a non-sewer but she's been at it non-stop since 1983. Quilting opened up a world of creativity where Dilys found she had a talent for color and design. A sympathetic teacher who brings out the best in her students, this accomplished author shares her clever dual image appliqué technique in this, her eighth book.

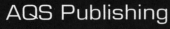